A Cultural History
of the
United States

—————————■—————————

Through the Decades

The 1980s

A Cultural History
of the
United States

∎

Through the Decades

The 1980s

Stuart A. Kallen

Lucent Books, Inc., San Diego, California

Library of Congress Cataloging-in-Publication Data

Kallen, Stuart A., 1955–
    The 1980s / by Stuart A. Kallen.
        p.   cm.—(A cultural history of the United States through
    the decades)
        Includes bibliographical references (p.   ) and index.
        Summary: Discusses the political, historical, and cultural life of
    the United States in the 1980s, including the end of communism, the
    Iran-Contra affair, and pop culture of the time.
        ISBN 1-56006-558-3 (lib. : alk. paper)
        1. United States—History—1969–   —Juvenile literature. 2. United
    States—Social life and customs—1971–   — Juvenile literature.
    3. Nineteen eighties—Juvenile literature. [1. United States—
    History—1969– 2. United States—Social life and customs—1971–
    3. Nineteen eighties.] I. Title. II. Series.
    E876.K343   1999
    973.92—dc21   98-28564
                                                                CIP
                                                                  AC

Copyright 1999 by Lucent Books, Inc.
P.O. Box 289011, San Diego, California 92198-9011

Printed in the U.S.A.

Contents

Introduction

Pictured from left to right are former presidents Jimmy Carter, Gerald Ford, and Richard Nixon at the 1978 funeral of former senator and 1968 Democratic presidential candidate Hubert Humphrey.

Summing Up the Seventies

The decade that lasted from 1980 to 1990 is remembered as the "go-go eighties." The reasons for that nickname are many. One of the most popular presidents in history sat in the White House. Big business—buoyed by government deregulation—gained stratospheric profits. Waves of business mergers rolled across the land as large companies gobbled up smaller ones. Computers, once pricey tools found mainly in offices and universities, became available to the average consumer. Television channels increased in number from four or five to almost sixty.

At the beginning of the decade, the United States was locked in ideological combat with the communist Soviet Union. By 1990, the Soviets had crumbled, capitalism won, and

Eastern Europe was free for the first time in sixty years.

Any summing up of the eighties, however, brings to light numerous contradictions. The popular president spent most of his second term fighting off disturbing scandals. Government deregulation precipitated a crisis in the savings and loan industry—one of the largest financial disasters in American history. In the midst of a period of soaring stock market prices, there were two prolonged recessions. While corporations merged and expanded, downsizing in several sectors of the economy caused high unemployment among average Americans. The collapse of communism was one of the greatest moments of the twentieth century. But for many in the former Soviet Union, life became confusing and harder than ever as crime ballooned and the economy headed for a crash. In the United States, television channels multiplied, but as Bruce Springsteen sang, "There's 57 channels and nothin' on!"[1]

Crisis in the Seventies

No decade can stand alone, and all of history is influenced by what went be-

Richard Nixon was forced to resign from the presidency after the Watergate scandal. Nixon's blatant lying left Americans less confident in their leaders.

fore. In many ways, the 1980s were heavily influenced by the 1970s, a period that began with Richard M. Nixon in the White House and Spiro T. Agnew as vice president. Nixon was a popular president first elected in 1968. He was reelected by a landslide in 1972. But during that election campaign, some of Nixon's advisers ordered a break-in at the Democratic party headquarters in Washington's Watergate apartment complex. The perpetrators were caught, and the trail of knowledge about the attempted burglary finally led to the president himself.

Meanwhile, Vice President Agnew was accused of having taken bribes while he was governor of Maryland in the late sixties. He resigned in 1973 and was replaced by Gerald Ford, a Republican congressman from Michigan. By 1974, Nixon faced certain impeachment for obstruction of justice and other charges in connection with attempts to cover up the Watergate break-in. He resigned, and Ford replaced him as president.

Politically and otherwise, the country was in terrible shape when Ford took office. Americans had come to realize that it was only a matter of time before the Vietnam War would be lost. In addition, shocked by the behavior of Nixon and his aides, people rapidly lost confidence in the U.S. government. Added to that were the economic troubles that combined stagnation with inflation, an unfavorable condition called "stagflation." Prices of food, energy, clothing, and housing rose quickly and steeply. Interest rates on home mortgages and car loans went up to 20 per-

cent—a threefold increase in less than a decade. While interest rates soared, the dollar bought less and less every day. Economists and average citizens feared another major depression like that of the 1930s.

Voters turned their wrath on Gerald Ford, and not only because of the economy. Ford had quickly issued full, free, and absolute pardon to former president Nixon. Democrat Jimmy Carter, a former governor of Georgia, emphasizing that he was a Washington outsider, beat Ford in the presidential race of 1976.

The Misery Index

Carter's administration was marked by disaster—much of it beyond the control of a U.S. president. The economy continued to flounder. Fuel prices continued to climb. Between 1975 and 1981 oil prices shot from $7.64 a barrel to $35.53 a barrel. An energy shortage created massive lines at gas stations, where people waited for hours to fill their tanks. The economy was so bad that a new term—the misery index—was invented to describe popular dissatisfaction with life in general. The combination of inflation and unemployment gave Americans of the late seventies the highest misery index seen in the country since the beginning of World War II.

Gerald Ford became president after Nixon's resignation but failed to win reelection. Many voters blamed Ford for the economic troubles plaguing the nation.

Union invaded Afghanistan in 1979, Carter stopped exports of grain and high-technology equipment to the Soviets. This angered farmers whose livelihood depended on selling excess grain to the Soviets. In April 1980, Carter announced that American athletes would not attend the summer Olympic Games in Moscow. This decision upset athletes, television executives, and millions of sports fans.

In 1978 conservative Islamic clergymen overthrew the U.S.-backed shah of Iran. On November 4, 1979, militants seized the U.S. embassy in Iran, taking sixty-three Americans hostage. Carter ordered a commando raid to free the hostages. The operation was a fiasco. Helicopters flying to the capital city of Tehran malfunctioned, killing eight American soldiers and wounding five. The hostage crisis dragged on for more than a year. Many Americans felt humiliated by this defeat and the blame fell squarely on Jimmy Carter. The Americans remained

Carter also had his share of foreign policy problems. When the Soviet

Three of the fifty-two American hostages released from Tehran arrive in Germany in 1981. The hostage crisis, which was one of the main reasons why President Jimmy Carter lost his bid for reelection, was resolved by Carter before Reagan's inauguration.

hostage in Iran for 444 days. They would be released minutes after the next president was sworn in on January 20, 1981.

Enter Reagan—Stage Right

In the midst of these disasters, Carter began his campaign for reelection. At the same time, actor-turned-governor-turned presidential candidate Ronald Wilson Reagan moved decisively into the national spotlight. Following a career in movies and television, Reagan had turned to politics. A well-known conservative Republican, he had run unsuccessfully against Nixon and Ford in his party's presidential primaries of 1968 and 1976.

Jimmy Carter told Americans that there were no simple solutions to their problems. Reagan, however, approached the political podium with a sunny and upbeat personality. As Bob Schieffer and Gary Paul Gates write in *The Acting President*:

> To an electorate that was now getting most of its information from the television, no one at first glance *looked* more like a President than the handsome, genial, former actor from California. Reagan oozed common sense and preached a simple message that challenged the oft-heard assumption that there are no simple answers in the modern world. "There *are* simple answers," he said.[2]

Reagan's telegenic qualities were legendary. As Larry Beinhart writes in *American Hero*:

> Reagan didn't work hard, he didn't know much about all those things that presidents are supposed to know—economics, foreign policy, law, history, even art. He did the opposite of what he said, seemed unable to tell truth from late-night TV, and should have been embarrassed by much of the company he kept. Yet he once again made the White House seem like a palace and the capital of a glittering imperium [empire]. Luck and blessing seemed to fall on all he did and there was a radiance around him.[3]

Reagan addressed an electorate that had been battered by Vietnam, Watergate, troubling social changes, and economic crises. Before they headed to the polls in November 1980, Reagan posed a question: "Just ask yourself, are you better off now that you were four years ago?" The voters answered with a resounding "No!" When the final votes were counted, out of the 86.5 million cast, the world learned that Reagan had received 51 percent, Carter 41 percent, and third-party candidate John Anderson 7 percent. Reagan's win in the electoral college was more dramatic. He carried 44 states with 489 electoral votes, to just 49 for Carter who carried only 6 states and the District of Columbia.

The election also gave the Republican party the opportunity of a lifetime. Republicans won both the White House and a majority in the Senate. It was the first time since 1953–1955 that the party had enjoyed majority status in the upper house. Combined with 192 Republicans and more than 30 avowedly conservative Democrats in the House of Representatives, Reagan would enjoy enough ideological support for a strong presidency.

From Actor to Politician: The Reagan Revolution

Ronald Reagan's life read like the script from a Hollywood movie. Born in Illinois in 1911, this son of a hard-drinking father and a religious mother learned to act in school plays. After college, he became a radio sports announcer in Des Moines, Iowa, where his smooth delivery attracted a large number of fans. He left for Hollywood in 1937 after a successful screen test. Soon, Reagan reached star status, portraying handsome American heroes in such movies as *International Squadron, Rear Gunner,* and *For God and Country.* When millions of men his age went to fight in World War II, Reagan enlisted in the Army Air Corps. But nearsightedness disqualified him from serving in combat. Instead he was assigned to the First Motion Picture Unit, where he acted in training films until the end of the war, in 1945.

Reagan's acting career fizzled after the war, but he served as president of his union, the Screen Actors Guild (SAG), from 1947 to 1952. During these postwar years, the Federal Bureau of Investigation (FBI) believed that some SAG members were or had been members of the tiny U.S. Communist party. Men and women who had gone to meetings of socialist or communist groups before the war soon found themselves being investigated. Reagan pledged cooperation with the FBI and worked as an informant. He also, however, used his position to clear some SAG members who had been wrongly accused. Although Reagan considered himself a political liberal, he took a conservative stance as SAG president. Reagan was committed to eliminating all traces of communism from the organization. To that end, according to David Wright in *America in the 20th Century,* "he helped blacklist some people associated with the motion picture business [for their political views.] As a result, no studio would use them for writing, acting, producing, or directing."[4]

The future president's conversion from liberal to conservative was completed when he went to work for General Electric. That industrial giant sponsored the *General Electric Theater* on television from 1953 to 1962. Reagan, who hosted the show, increasingly became a defender of corporate America. His second wife, Nancy Davis Reagan, was from a conservative family, and her views also played a role in Reagan's conversion.

When Ronald Reagan arrived in Hollywood in 1937, he was an unmarried Democrat who had never been very much involved in politics. By 1964 he was a married father of four who was hosting *Death Valley Days* on television and devoting his spare energy to the Republican party. As one of his assignments, he spoke at a fund-raiser for Republican presiden-

Ronald Reagan plays Knute Rockne in this 1940 film still. After a somewhat unsuccessful acting career, Reagan became interested in politics.

carried on nationwide television, several California businessmen approached Reagan with the suggestion that he run for governor.

In his autobiography, *An American Life,* Reagan writes about the beliefs set forth in his speeches at that time:

> I recounted [to the audience] the relentless expansion of the federal government, the proliferation of government bureaucrats who were taking control of American business, and criticized the liberal Democrats for taking the country down the road to socialism. As usual, I included some examples of Americans whose business or personal lives had been tormented by bureaucrats and cited examples of government waste.[5]

In the campaign against the incumbent, Democrat Edmund G. Brown, Reagan railed against welfare cheats and antiwar protesters on the college campuses. Although he was dismissed

tial candidate Barry Goldwater. After that appeal, an articulate performance by his opponent as "just an actor," Reagan won the governorship of California. His million-vote margin of victory was more than any candidate for that office had received up until that time.

The new governor accomplished his main goals of welfare and education reform, while holding down the size of state government, and he was elected for a second term in 1970. He had long had his eye on the top national office, however, and in 1980 he finally received the Republican party's nomination. Then, on November 4, 1980, at the age of sixty-nine, he became the oldest man to be elected president of the United States.

When Ronald Reagan became the nation's fortieth president, press and pundits hailed the new era as the "Reagan revolution."

Chapter One

Former movie actor and governor of California Ronald Reagan reaches out to a sea of hands during his 1980 campaign for the presidency.

The Reagan Revolution

Reagan had declared during the campaign that if elected, he would make the economy his first priority. Once in office, he moved quickly to make good on that promise. One month after his inauguration, Reagan presented a plan to Congress that would scale back the growth of government and return billions of tax dollars to workers and businesses. In a prime-time televised address, he said: "If we don't do this, [cut taxes and trim the size of the federal government], inflation and a growing tax burden will put an end to everything we believe in and to our dreams for the future." But he stressed that the nation's economic problems easily could be cured. "We are in control here," he said. "There is nothing wrong with America that—together—we can't fix."[6]

Reagan's proposed budget cut spending by $41.4 billion and slashed personal and business taxes by $53.9 billion. With these cuts, Reagan predicted a $45 billion budget deficit. Combined with a reduction in the "explosion" of business regulations, Reagan claimed that his budget and tax reductions would cause the economy to grow and inflation to plummet. His goals were summarized by members of the *Congressional Quarterly* staff as follows:

Such a growth in savings—spurred on by tax cuts—would free as much as $44 billion in new funds for investment. That, in turn would improve productivity, provide more jobs, and bring down prices.[7]

The president also maintained that his policies would leave in place a "social safety net," for the truly needy. He recommended a funding increase in only one department—Defense. The package submitted by Reagan was by far the most ambitious government scale-back ever proposed by a president.

Critics of the president charged that an across-the-board income tax reduction would benefit well-to-do Americans more than anyone else. House Speaker Thomas P. O'Neill Jr., when asked if there were inequities in Reagan's package replied, "You bet there are. It is important that the sacrifices called for in the projected budget are shared equally and the benefits of the tax cut are not reaped primarily by the few."[8]

The keystone of Reagan's economic plan was called "supply-side economics," which is based on the idea that if corporations and the wealthy are taxed less, they will spend more money, buoy the economy, and help pay off the federal budget deficit. Those in lower economic brackets are supposed to benefit from the additional jobs created and the cheaper goods that were expected to be available. Critics called this theory "trickle-down economics." Others called the plan "Reaganomics."

Cutting the Budget

President Reagan chose David A. Stockman, a young, conservative two-term Republican representative from Michigan, as the director of the Office of Budget Management (OMB). Stockman acknowledged that he had "long sought a chance to arrest the growth of the federal government's social pork barrel."[9] Stockman's commitment to reduce the government's monetary involvement in all walks of American life was to make him one of the most active budget directors in history. In Congress, Stockman had worked to oppose new government entitlement programs,

Director of the Budget David Stockman answers questions about the Reagan budget, claiming it would be impossible to build up defenses, grant tax cuts, and balance the federal budget.

and when he took over the reins of OMB, he had an inch-thick list of spending cuts he promised to use to balance the budget.

However, in 1981, Stockman made a startling confession: "that the President's vaunted supply-side economic program was not only based on

questionable premises, and that it didn't work."[10] In an article that appeared in the *Atlantic Monthly* magazine, Stockman said that budget cuts amounting to $100 billion a year would be required to offset the increases in defense spending that the president proposed to pair with substantial tax cuts. Stockman said Reagan's proposals would "hurt millions of people in the short run, abruptly severing the umbilical cords of dependency that ran from Washington to every nook and cranny of the nation." That is, the budget director saw the failure of supply-side theory as a chance to terminate many social welfare programs. New York democratic Senator Daniel P. Moynihan, however, charged that Reagan's plan "consciously and deliberately brought about higher deficits to force domestic cuts."[11]

In the *Atlantic Monthly* article Stockman also revealed that he and other economic advisers had seen alarming projections that showed huge deficits ranging from $82 billion in 1982 to $116 billion by 1984.

Stockman's predictions turned out to be correct. During Reagan's eight years in office, budget deficits increased more than fourfold, from $35 billion in 1980 to $155 billion in 1988. High budget deficits would become one of the main political topics throughout the eighties and early nineties.

President Reagan was called the Great Communicator for his easy manner on TV. Because he was able to effectively relate his message to millions of Americans, his budget had popular support and was quickly approved by Congress in 1981. It included a major tax cut, $43 billion in budget cuts in domestic programs, and cutbacks in regulations that affected business and the environment.

Reagan's budget did get the economy moving again. And his optimism and can-do attitude increased public confidence when he made sweeping statements like "There are no such things as limits to growth, because there are no limits on the human capacity for intelligence, imagination and wonder."[12]

Surviving Assassination

President Reagan had just taken office when he was shot by a young man named John Hinckley. On March 30, 1981, a .22 caliber bullet punctured Reagan's lung and lodged near his heart, but he miraculously survived. Many Americans breathed a sigh of relief when the president was seen waving and smiling from his hospital window a few days after the shooting.

The assassination attempt did not change the president's view on gun control. Bill Adler quotes the president in *The Uncommon Wisdom of Ronald Reagan:*

> My position has always been clear—I believe that law-abiding citizens have a right to bear arms. I believe, too, that within that right comes a responsibility to use guns safely and within compliance with the law. . . .
>
> So I believe . . . that we should concentrate on increasing the penalties for those who use guns to commit crime.

Secret Service agents rush to help a police officer and presidential press secretary James Brady who were wounded after John Hinckley attempted to assassinate the president in 1981.

The assassination attempt made Reagan even more popular, giving him the public image of a man who could not be stopped by bullets. Able to return to work within a few weeks, the president was warmly received by his fellow Republicans and by opposition Democrats alike.

Still, the numbers were mixed. Inflation dropped below 10 percent, but unemployment in 1982 was the highest in forty years. By the summer of 1982, the federal budget deficit was threatening to surpass $200 billion. Reluctantly, the president and leading Republicans agreed to tax increases totaling $98.3 billion. The tax package raised federal taxes on telephone service and increased corporate withholding taxes, airplane ticket taxes, social security taxes, and other fees paid to the government.

In 1983 the economic picture brightened, with a resurgent stock market, low inflation, and rising production. Recovery was menaced by large budget deficits, but the jobless rate continued to inch downward.

Welfare Cuts

More controversial than tax cuts were the Reagan administration's proposals for limiting such federal social programs as Aid to Families with Dependent Children (AFDC) and food stamps, on which millions of poor Americans relied.

The roots of welfare run deep in American society. Federal aid to the poor began during the Great Depression in the 1930s, under President Franklin D. Roosevelt's New Deal programs. Care for children, the aged, the

sick, and the distressed was dramatically increased in the 1960s under President Lyndon B. Johnson's War on Poverty. By 1980 the numbers of these programs, and their costs, had spiraled higher and higher.

When Reagan was elected, programs for the poor made up about 10 percent of the federal budget. They included AFDC, Medicaid (medical care for the poor), Supplemental Security Income for the aged and disabled poor, free school meals, financial aid to be applied to fuel bills, low-income housing, job and education programs, legal services, food supplements for pregnant women, infants, and children under five (WIC), and social services for the poor.

Welfare reform, however, had been one of the main planks in Reagan's 1980 campaign. In an interview with the Detroit *News* in January 1980, he said:

I think one of the big things wrong with welfare today—and there is much wrong with it—(is that) if welfare were truly successful, (government) would be boasting each year of how much it has reduced the welfare rolls, how many less people there were in need of assistance. Now remember . . . we're not talking about those people who are invalid and through no fault of their own cannot provide for themselves. We have always taken care of those people—and always will. We're talking about those people who are able-bodied and who, for whatever reason—it may be lack of skill or whatever—have not been able to make their way out there in the competitive world. So the idea of welfare should be to put those people back on their feet, make them self-supporting and independent.[13]

To shrink welfare spending, Congress passed Reagan's Reconciliation Act of 1981 which reduced the budgets of 212 federal programs. Some entitlement programs were hard to change. There were no reductions in Social Security payments, to avoid having the political strength of older Americans turn against the Republicans. Similarly, huge Medicare expenses were difficult to reduce because doing so would have threatened the quality of health care for the elderly. Pensions for government workers and the military—a large sum—were also untouchable for political reasons. This meant that the reductions had to come from other areas of the budget. These other areas turned out to involve many programs focused mostly on the poor, especially the working poor.

The cuts made in Congress for low-income people in 1982 included 11 percent in food stamps, 28 percent in child nutrition programs, 13 percent in AFDC, 25 percent in student financial aid, and 28 percent in fuel assistance to the poor. Putting the cuts in human terms, one report announced that Reagan's 1982 budget reduced:

income, in-kind benefits, or public service jobs from between 20 and 25 million people who live just above the poverty line. . . . By the fall of 1982. . . . 660,000 children had lost Medicaid; 1 million people had lost food stamps, and food stamp benefits had been reduced for another 20 million. About 365,000 families with dependent children had lost their monthly checks, and the AFDC checks had been reduced for another 260,000 families. About 3.2 million children no longer participated in the school lunch program; about 750,000 children lost their eligibility for school lunches, and 500,000 children had been dropped from the summer meals program.[14]

The battles over these budget cuts filled newspapers and television screens for two years. Reagan's proposals were heavily criticized by Democrats. New York governor Mario Cuomo, who opposed Reagan's cuts in social programs, delivered an impassioned speech at the 1984 Democratic convention: "Reagan made the denial of compassion acceptable and did it in such a wonderfully svelte way. Reagan gave the middle class a reason not to care about the poor because they would waste it anyway. . . . Welfare was a rip-off. . . . Reagan convinced Americans—and they wanted to be convinced."[15]

Other Americans supported the cuts because they believed welfare should be

One of Reagan's objectives was to cut federal programs for the poor, which greatly affected children. Here, a six-year-old girl waits while her mother prepares the watered-down stew that will be the family's only meal for the day.

The Teflon President

Over the years, Reagan became known as the Teflon president, because it appeared that his critics' charges never stuck to him. Bob Schieffer writes about this phenomenon in *The Acting President:*

> Reagan had a special knack for telling stories about American heroes. One [World War II] yarn he told on several occasions: "The young ball-turret gunner was wounded, and they couldn't get him out of the B-17 turret there while flying. . . . The last man to leave saw the commander sit down on the floor. He took the boy's hand and said, 'Never mind, son, we'll ride it down together.' Congressional Medal of Honor, posthumously awarded." A reporter combed through all the citations for all 434 Medals of Honor and could not find that particular story. He did, however, come up with a possible source: a 1944 movie called *Wing and a Prayer*. When he saw that film, Reagan filed it away in his memory. Then at some point over the years, he came to believe that it was a real event in a real war.

Reagan frequently misspoke in public, and many believed that he deliberately distorted the truth when he felt that another version of reality would be helpful. The public generally chose to shrug off such gaffs, however. Thus reports of flaws in his character or judgment, which would have been severely damaging to the reputation of an ordinary politician, made little impact on the popular perception of the president. The majority of Americans continued to like him, and he enjoyed considerable support no matter what he said.

temporary help to people in need, not a permanent payment to people who did not want to work.

Military Policy and the Defense Buildup

While economic and social policies were enacted quickly, the Reagan administration's defense buildup took place over the course of several years. Reagan's military policies were guided by his unwavering dislike of the communist system as practiced in the Soviet Union. His hard-line approach to the USSR had changed little since the 1950s and he believed that the Soviets "have never retreated from their Marxist dream of one communist world."[16]

Defense was an issue throughout the 1980 campaign and Reagan believed that the Soviet Union had surpassed the United States as a military power. Thus he reasoned that if the country was to arrange arms reductions with the Soviet Union, it was necessary first to achieve a position of great strength.

Throughout his political career, Reagan spoke of the evils of the communist system, emphasizing the Soviets' stated goal of world domination. He was sure that the Soviet leaders respected strength and that a U.S. military buildup would force the Soviets to reduce their nuclear arsenal. To regain the superiority believed necessary to secure an advantageous negotiating position, the Reagan administration initiated a costly military buildup that markedly increased the nation's nuclear capability.

Reagan approved plans for deploying MX missiles (he called them Peacekeepers), a strategic weapon that targeted the Soviet Union. He pressed ahead with the Carter administration's plan to put medium-range nuclear missiles in Europe. These cruise missiles were meant to counter the recently deployed SS-20 missiles of the Soviet Union. Reagan advocated the construction of the Strategic Defense Initiative (SDI), popularly known as Star Wars, as a high-tech antimissile system designed to protect the United States from nuclear attack. He also approved development of the superelusive stealth bomber.

In 1981, to achieve the goal of mounting a credible threat to the Soviets, the Reagan administration budgeted $108.3 billion for defense over the next six years.

Shifting Values

On domestic issues, President Reagan's views reflected his conservative philosophy. He opposed abortion, was against the decriminalization of marijuana, and maintained that the courts had become too lenient toward criminals. The president supported the death penalty and opposed stricter forms of gun control. He often complained of a "virus of permissiveness [that] spreads its deadly poison." [17]

Reagan had strong backing from those who make up what is now called the Christian right—devout, politically conservative Christians. "Not a churchgoer himself, Reagan crusaded for the conservative themes the evangelists loved, such as outlawing abortion and stamping out pornography." [18]

The power of the Pentecostalists, Fundamentalists, and charismatic Christians was boosted considerably in the late seventies. At that time the Federal Communications Commission decided that television stations could fulfill their public-service duties by carrying religious programming. By the eighties, televangelists like Jim and Tammy Bakker, Jerry Falwell, and Pat Robertson were raising millions of dollars a day using television as their pulpit. Televangelists got the attention of many economically troubled Americans who were puzzled by an increasingly complex modern society.

Jerry Falwell was by far the most successful of the religious broadcasters.

Demanding a Nuclear Freeze

Reagan's arms buildup did not go unnoticed among young Americans. On June 12, 1982, there were huge antinuclear protests across the United States. Writers for the Associated Press filed many reports on these events, as typified by the following excerpt from *The Reagan Era: 1981–1988.*

More than 550,000 protesters from as far away as Hiroshima rallied in Central Park [in New York City] on Saturday to demand a nuclear weapons freeze in the biggest political demonstration in U.S. history. But [Secretary of Defense] Caspar Weinberger indicated that the large turnout was unlikely to have direct impact on administration policy.

A group of 50 counterdemonstrators, led by fundamentalist Rev. Carl McIntire marched outside of Central Park chanting, "Go march in Moscow," and "Freeze now, fry later."

In San Francisco, meanwhile, about 30,000 people rallied for a nuclear freeze Saturday, and smaller gatherings were held in several other cities from Boise, Idaho, to Augusta, Maine.

Leslie Cagen, a spokeswoman for the rally said the 130 groups who planned the event "represented constituencies that historically [had] not worked together." But on Saturday, "We found the common concern. We found the common fear. And we found the common commitment. That's why we're able to draw this many people."

Protesters participate in a rally in New York City to show their support for a nuclear weapons freeze. Reagan opposed any kind of arms reductions, believing that a strong military was the only way America could regain its international reputation.

[In a concert at the New York event] Jackson Browne was joined on stage by Bruce Springsteen, Joan Baez, Linda Ronstadt, and James Taylor.

The estimate by police of 550,000 made Saturday's gathering the largest rally in New York's history and the largest disarmament rally ever in the nation.

He created a political organization called the Moral Majority and became the unofficial chaplain of the Republican White House. By publicly condemning certain politicians, the Moral Majority defeated several Democratic officeholders on the national level. The organization later became the Christian Coalition, which was very influential in Republican politics well into the nineties.

Four More Years: Reagan's Second Term

Reagan's deficit spending and defense buildup boosted the economy. Interest rates fell, inflation subsided, and Americans were helped by a congressional jobs bill. Democrats nominated Walter Mondale, who had been Jimmy Carter's vice president, to run against Reagan in 1984. Mondale promised Americans that, if elected, he would raise taxes to lower the deficit. This position made him fantastically unpopular. In the election, Reagan won in every state except Mondale's home state of Minnesota. At the age of seventy-three, Reagan was sworn in for his second term.

When revelations emerged that the president had been willing to subvert the Constitution in what would become known as the Iran-Contra scandal of 1986, his popularity declined in

Ronald Reagan received tremendous support from religious conservatives, including the Reverend Jerry Falwell (pictured), creator of the political organization called the Moral Majority.

many quarters. The 1986 congressional elections saw Democrats gain in both houses. As Reagan's two terms in office came to an end, CBS reporter Bob Schieffer offered his opinion of the president's administration:

The widely held view as Reagan left office was that his legacy was one of good news and bad news. He was widely praised for reviving the nation's morale and for driving down inflation and unemployment. But many said that the feeling of economic well-being rested precariously on a mountain of debt, the enormous deficits that resulted from his economic policy.

We should not make too little of the way that Reagan's indomitable good humor and confidence revived the nation's confidence in the presidency. Indeed, it was a measure of just how low expectations of the presidency had fallen that toward the end of Reagan's term, some of the commentators were congratulating him for simply finishing his assignment in good humor and health. For the first time since the Eisenhower era, a president had not been conquered by the office that he held.[19]

President Reagan was beloved by millions of people. But his hands-off management style left many administrators operating with little supervision from the top. This led to a rash of scandals in the late 1980s that overshadowed the final years of the Reagan presidency.

Before the end of Reagan's two terms, over two hundred members of his administration had been indicted for various crimes. But the scandal

known as Iran-Contra overshadowed all the other investigations.

In a series of complicated maneuvers involving several countries, the United States sold weapons to Iran. Americans were shocked when they learned of the scandal because Reagan had given dozens of speeches calling Iran a rogue nation and a terrorist state. Profits from the weapons sale were used to fund a CIA-backed army in Nicaragua. This was done secretly, in direct opposition to the will of Congress.

Trouble in Nicaragua: Iran-Contra, Part 1

In July 1979 the corrupt Nicaraguan dictator Anastasio Somoza was overthrown by a broad-based coalition that soon came to be dominated by its military arm, the Cuban-backed Sandinistas. Once in power, the Sandinistas disappointed supporters of the revolution by turning toward communism and turning against the free press, the Catholic Church, and intellectuals who criticized them.

Among the first Nicaraguans to present an organized opposition to the Sandinistas were former Somoza partisans and National Guard members who became known as Contras. But if the ruling Sandinistas were generally unpopular, the Contras were feared. Nicaraguans remembered all too well

Corrupt Nicaraguan dictator Anastasio So-moza was overthrown in 1979 by leftist guer-rillas called Sandinistas. Reagan strongly op-posed the Sandinista regime, believing it would pose a leftist threat to America's footing in North America.

the excesses of Somoza's violence-prone troops.

In the early eighties, the Contras, eager to regain power, were gearing up for a guerrilla war against the Sandinistas. U.S. opinion leaned toward keeping out of any such conflict. Thus, Congress, knowing of the president's fierce opposition to communism in all its forms, wanted to block any attempt

by Contra sympathizers in the CIA and in the military to bring about the over-throw of the elected government of Nicaragua. In May 1982 the House of Representatives voted overwhelmingly to ban the Pentagon and the CIA from providing weapons or training to anti-Sandinista forces intent on toppling the Sandinista regime. This law became known as the Boland Amendment, af-ter its author, Massachusetts represen-tative Edward Boland.

Despite the official ban on U.S. aid, however, the Contras were able to wage war against their fellow countrymen, of-ten operating from bases in neighboring Honduras. Strong suspicions of U.S. as-sistance to the Contras were confirmed dramatically in October 1986 when Sandinistas shot down a C-123 cargo plane carrying rifles, ammunition, rocket-propelled grenades, and jungle boots over Nicaragua. One crew mem-ber survived the crash, pilot Eugene Hasenfus, a forty-five-year-old former marine. Hasenfus cooperated with his captors, who also seized papers and log-books from the downed aircraft. When Hasenfus told the Sandinistas his under-standing of his assignment—that he had been employed by the CIA to deliver arms destined for the Contras—there was a great public outcry.

The Reagan administration issued strong negative responses to all questions

Eugene Hasenfus sits surrounded by arms that were recovered from his plane after it was shot down and he was captured by the Sandinistas. Hasenfus was part of an illegal plot to give arms to anti-Sandinista guerrillas.

about the role of the United States in the aborted mission:

> "I'm glad you asked. Absolutely not," Reagan replied when asked if there was any U.S. involvement whatsoever. . . . There was "no connection at all," said [Secretary of State George P.] Shultz. "No government agencies, none" were involved, said [Assistant Secretary of State] Elliott Abrams.[20]

Two weeks after the shoot down, the House Judiciary Committee asked Attorney General Edwin P. Meese III to appoint an independent counsel to investigate several key players, including William Casey, the director of the CIA, and Oliver North, a marine lieutenant colonel who appeared to be closely linked to the operation.

The fighting in Nicaragua continued until 1988, when the Contras and the Sandinistas signed a cease-fire. But while the civil war was raging in Central America, the Reagan administration was engaged in a different kind of war in the Mideast.

Running a War from the White House Basement: Iran-Contra, Part 2

In 1985 and 1986 Reagan administration officials secretly supplied shoulder-fired antitank missiles to Iran, which was in the midst of a long, bloody conflict with its neighbor Iraq, also a recipient of U.S. arms aid. This action violated an embargo on arms sales that had been in place since the Iran hostage crisis of 1979–1981. But the Reagan administration hoped that Iran would help obtain the release of American hostages being held by Islamic militants in Lebanon. To offer such a bribe was contrary to long-standing American policy of not negotiating with terrorists for the release of hostages. Nevertheless,

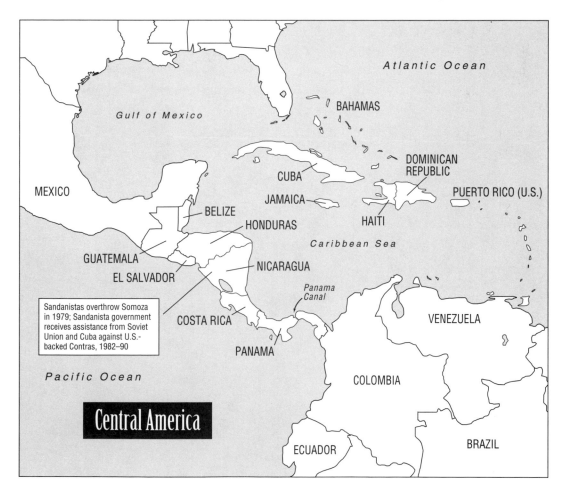

Sandanistas overthrow Somoza in 1979; Sandanista government receives assistance from Soviet Union and Cuba against U.S.-backed Contras, 1982–90

Central America

profits from these illegal arms sales were transferred to the Contra rebels, a violation of the spirit, if not the letter, of the Boland Amendment.

By 1986, the nerve center for the illegal operations that came to be known as Iran-Contra was the office of Oliver North in the White House basement. A member of the National Security Council (NSC), North oversaw the arms sales to Iran and arranged to divert the money to the Contras. Already imperiled by the revelations that had emerged from the confession of Hasenfus, the downed C-123 pilot, North's operation blew apart completely before the year was

out. In November, reports of U.S. arms sales to Iran, first published in an obscure Arabic-language newspaper in Beirut, broke in the American press.

The president went on TV and "gave a confused explanation of his administration's Iran policy."[21] But he assured the country that there would be no more dealings with Iran. Meanwhile, Attorney General Meese, who was investigating the Contra scandal, uncovered the connection between illegal arms sales in the Mideast and funneling of funds to the Nicaraguan guerrillas.

In the uproar that followed, a special prosecutor was appointed. CIA

The Middle East

United States sells arms to Iran and uses funds to support Contras in Nicaragua, 1985-86

director Casey died before he could be questioned under oath, but Oliver North was among those called on to explain their actions. North's testimony, which implicated the president, the attorney general, and the director of the CIA, concluded with admissions of error, falsehood, obstruction of justice, and destruction of evidence—all for a higher cause.

Dressed in his marine uniform, his chest covered with campaign ribbons and decorations from his service in Vietnam, North gave a riveting performance. But although much of the country was in the grip of "Olliemania," the witness antagonized the special prosecutor, former judge Lawrence Walsh, by his refusal to apologize for what he had done.

Oliver North is sworn in to testify before the Iran-Contra Committee. The televised hearings showed North quietly unrepentant as he argued that he was just following orders.

Wrapping up the Scandal

Belatedly, in April 1989, Oliver North was put on trial. Facing twelve felony charges, he stated under oath that he had been ordered by superiors to keep silent about his role in the matters. He named Reagan's vice president, George Bush, who had become president in January, as an intermediary in the secret effort to arm the Contras. North received a relatively light sentence; he

appealed, and after the second trial, the charges were dropped. Also tried was the man who had headed the NSC while North was there. Former admiral John Poindexter received a heavier sentence, which was also successfully appealed.

Subpoenaed to testify at Poindexter's trial in 1990, former president Reagan recalled very little of the affair:

There had been so many meetings; 80 a day, someone had told him. There had been so many pieces of paper; 50 million at least, generated during his eight years as president. He remembered almost nothing. Gamely, his questioners tried to encourage him. Perhaps he remembered the meeting about Iran in August 1985 when he was in the hospital. No, nothing; or else the memory of a meeting, "but I can't recall what the outcome was or what we were discussing."

With Contra policy, matters became vaguer still. Reagan was shown a picture of [Contra leader Adolfo] Calero meeting him in the Oval Office; he did not know who he was. He had not read the Tower Commission's report; did not know that [National Security Advisor Robert] McFarlane had pleaded guilty to misdemeanors; did not know the substance of the charges against Poindexter.[22]

With the Sandinistas out of power in Nicaragua, and the powerful Soviet Union in disarray, the Iran-Contra scandal quickly faded from the headlines.

In 1988 Vice President George Bush ran for president with J. Danforth Quayle as his running mate. Bush was elected and sworn in on January 20, 1989.

When George Bush took office, Ronald and Nancy Reagan left Wash-

After his two terms in office, Ronald Reagan left the presidency with high public approval. Many still revere and admire the former president.

ington for retirement in California. Reagan's approval ratings were the highest of any president since World War II. But over the course of the decade, the national debt had climbed from $900 billion to over $2 trillion. Investors in foreign countries provided much of the capital to pay for this debt, an economic fact of life that transformed the United States from the world's leading lender nation to the world's number-one debtor. Over $400 billion was owed abroad when Reagan left office. The interest on this money alone became the second largest expenditure in the budget, after defense.

Reagan's conservative views shifted the political dialogue to the right. The federal government, however, was no smaller at the end of Reagan's tenure than at the start. Reagan's popularity survived, however, because of his leadership style that stressed confidence and a positive outlook. In 1994 it was announced that the former president was suffering from Alzheimer's disease.

Chapter Two

A unit of Soviet soldiers march in Red Square in Moscow in July 1987 on the seventieth anniversary of the Russian Revolution.

Final Curtain on Communism

Ronald Reagan oversaw one of the largest peacetime defense build-ups in the history of the United States. This costly U.S. effort, in turn, forced the Soviet Union into an expensive arms race that it could hardly afford. The country had been running on empty, having had three ineffective leaders in a matter of three years. Sky-rocketing energy prices that shook the West also threatened the Soviet's un-wieldy economic and social system. When the system of totalitarian com-munism fell in 1989, it was one of the most dramatic historical events since the end of World War II.

On November 9, 1989, thousands of people assembled at the wall that the Soviets had erected between West and East Germany in 1961. They gathered with hammers, chisels, sledgehammers, and crowbars. In three days, with the relentless pounding of ten thousand people, the concrete structure known as the Berlin Wall came tumbling down. For the first time since the end of World War II, communist East Germany was physically united with free republican West Germany. As a thousand camera flashbulbs bathed the night in an unearthly blue glow, the "iron curtain" around Czechoslovakia, Hungary, Poland, Yugoslavia, Romania, Bulgaria, and other regions dominated by the Communist party of the USSR began to crumble away into history.

The collapse of the Soviet Union was the biggest victory for freedom and democracy since the end of World War II.

This man is one of thousands who took aim at the Berlin Wall in 1989.

In the United States, some credited the hard-line anticommunist policies of

President Reagan for the Soviet collapse. Others pointed to the weaknesses inherent in the Soviet economic system. Former Soviet general Oleg Kalugin said, "American policy of the 1980s was a catalyst for the collapse of the Soviet Union."[23]

Deputy secretary of state in the Clinton administration, Strobe Talbot, offers another perspective:

> The difference from the [Soviet] standpoint between a conservative Republican administration and a liberal Democratic administration was not that great. The Soviet Union collapsed: the Cold War ended almost overwhelmingly because of internal contradictions or pressures within the Soviet Union and the Soviet system itself. And even if Jimmy Carter had been re-elected and been followed by Walter Mondale, something like what we have now seen probably would have happened.[24]

As with most major historical turnarounds, the truth undoubtedly lies somewhere in between. The Soviet Union was facing a host of problems when it collapsed.

Changing Soviet Leaders

During the first four years of the Reagan presidency, the U.S. chief executive did not once meet with a leader of the Soviet Union. This was because of the great mortality rate at that country's highest levels of power. Three Soviet leaders—Leonid Brezhnev, Yuri Andropov, and Konstantin Chernenko—died between 1982 and 1985.

Brezhnev had held high office in the USSR from the early 1960s; he was party chief and president at the time of his death in November 1982. Brezhnev had been in poor health for years—he had suffered two strokes and doctors had twice declared him dead. But under Brezhnev, the Soviets had achieved military parity with the United States. Moscow's influence extended to Laos, Cambodia, Ethiopia, Angola, Mozambique, and other countries.

When Brezhnev died, Yuri Andropov—head of the KGB and a member of the ruling Politburo—became the new head, or general secretary, of the Communist party. Andropov was also the first Soviet leader to announce that strict communist ideology would never bring the USSR into the modern world.

In the early eighties, Soviet relations with the United States had reached an all-time low. As the Reagan administration's $108 billion defense buildup proceeded, the president addressed the National Association of Evangelicals, which represented thirty-eight thousand churches and 3.5 million people. In his speech Reagan said the antinuclear

KGB director Yuri Andropov succeeded Leonid Brezhnev as head of the Soviet Union in 1982. Unhealthy from the start, Andropov quickly succumbed to illness, dying in 1984.

pire bent on aggression" and denounced totalitarian states as "the focus of evil in the modern world."[25]

The Soviets reacted to the "evil empire" speech by calling Reagan a "power-thirsty lunatic about to blow up the world."[26] The exchange of heated words made headlines across the globe. The Soviets then threatened to put new missiles in Eastern Europe. They also said they would assume a "launch on warning" posture: that is, Soviet computers would launch Soviet nuclear missiles instantly if the computers perceived a threat.

Russian Roulette

While the superpower war of words was being played out, Andropov lay in a hospital, gravely ill. Few people knew that he had only one kidney. As they had done to conceal the condition of the ailing Brezhnev, Soviet propaganda experts pieced together film footage of the bedridden Andropov to give the impression that he was still in control and able to work. Meanwhile, an ambitious Politburo member named Mikhail Gorbachev was covering Andropov's duties. Then, on February 10, 1984, having disappeared from public for 175 days, Andropov died. By the time of his funeral four days

movement was a "very dangerous fraud," and that the United States and the USSR were "locked in a struggle between right and wrong, good and evil." He called the Soviet Union an "evil em-

War in Grenada

The anticommunist feelings of Ronald Reagan were not confined to the Soviet Union. The administration also feared communism in America's "backyard." The tiny Caribbean island of Grenada, near the north coast of Venezuela, is home to about eighty thousand people. In October 1983, a violent left-wing regime took over the government. They killed the prime minister, Maurice Bishop, imposed a shoot-on-sight curfew, and were threatening about one thousand Americans on the island. Furthermore, they had accepted aid and advisers from nearby communist Cuba. Other islands in the region were alarmed and pleaded with the United States to restore peace and stability.

On October 25, 1983, about nineteen hundred U.S. Army Rangers and U.S. Marines invaded Grenada. About six hundred Cubans and thirty Soviet military personnel were quickly captured. The main force was followed by about three hundred troops from six Caribbean nations. Three Cubans were killed and twenty-two wounded.

Whether Reagan had the authority to take action in Grenada has been debated. The Constitution says that only Congress has the right to make war. President Reagan had given no indication to Congress, the press, or the public that the marines were going to invade Grenada. But because the action was over within a week, there were few casualties, and it was popular with the American people, Grenada's legalities were never investigated.

As Chernenko spoke at Andropov's funeral, it was obvious that another sick old man would be running the Soviet Union. The new general secretary slurred his words and wheezed in the frigid air, mumbling complaints about his late predecessor.

Like his counterpart in Washington, Chernenko was, at seventy-two, the oldest man to lead his nation. Unlike Reagan, Chernenko was teetering on the edge of death. After thirteen months of pushing Brezhnev's tired old policies, Chernenko died on March 10, 1985. It was the third death of a Soviet general secretary in as many years. On March 12, Mikhail Gorbachev was announced as the new leader of the Soviet Communist party.

Changing of the Guard

Months before Gorbachev became party secretary, he had visited Great Britain, where he became the focus of the Western media. Gorbachev exuded charm, poise, and intelligence—the first two qualities rarely seen in a Soviet leader. Under the bright lights of the press, Gorbachev seemed a man in control. And "Gorbi," as he was called, was accompanied by his wife, Raisa. From the moment Mrs. Gorbachev

later, Chernenko had been named party general secretary.

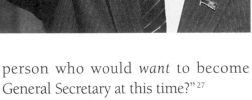

Konstantin Chernenko (above) succeeded Andropov as president of the Soviet Union but, like Andropov, died soon after taking office. Chernenko's successor, Mikhail Gorbachev (right), was revolutionary in many ways: He was relatively young and thoroughly supported economic reform.

stepped off the airplane, the press swooned over her natural charisma, glamour, and intelligence. It was obvious that the couple represented a new Soviet generation who talked, behaved, and dressed in a way that Westerners could understand.

Gorbachev did not seem to be a power-hungry man. After he rose to the top of Soviet government, he told a close friend, "Can you believe there is a person who would *want* to become General Secretary at this time?"[27]

Gorbachev was speaking of the massive problems facing the Soviet Union. There were shortages of everything, from food and clothing to housing. The system was so inefficient and corrupt that, according to reports by the Associated Press, three out of four Soviet-grown potatoes rotted in the field. Average Soviet citizens were

Mideast Troubles

The saber rattling of the superpowers was often driven off the front pages by problems in the Mideast. In 1982 Israel invaded Lebanon, beginning a chain of events that had tragic consequences for the United States. As the fighting escalated, American troops were dispatched to the Lebanese capital of Beirut. On October 23, 1983, a suicide bomber rammed a pickup truck packed with explosives into an airport building full of sleeping marines. The four-story structure blew up, killing at least 241 marines and wounding 115.

The marines soon departed from Lebanon, but radical Moslems continued in their fierce resentment of U.S. support for Israel. In March 1985, six American reporters including Terry Anderson, were taken hostage in Lebanon. In June, two gunmen in Beirut seized a TWA jetliner with more than a hundred Americans aboard and killed an American passenger. Other passengers were held hostage for seventeen days. On October 7, Palestinian hijackers seized an Italian cruise liner,

An aerial view of the American embassy in Beirut after it was bombed by terrorists. Combating such terrorism became a major focus of Reagan's administration.

Achille Lauro, at sea near Egypt. There were more than four hundred people aboard, but the terrorists seized a sixty-nine-year-old Jewish American man named Leon Klinghoffer. The wheelchair-bound Klinghoffer was shot and killed, then pushed over the side of the ship into the sea.

spending one-third of their waking hours standing in lines at shops to buy basic goods such as food and clothing.

Gorbachev plunged into the new job as no other general secretary had before. He had a personality ideally suited to television. His charisma on Soviet television—and on Western

TV—quickly made him something of a worldwide celebrity. Gorbachev was embarrassed by the Soviet propaganda machinery that had elevated earlier leaders to godlike status. More important, Gorbachev ordered physical examinations for all top officials. Many prominent figures in the Kremlin were seventy, eighty, or ninety years old. Gorbachev let it be known that he wanted healthy and vigorous people in charge. Those who were not physically fit were forced to retire.

The new secretary general amazed everyone by spending his days touring Moscow's schools, factories, hospitals, markets, and apartments. He was mobbed by loving crowds wanting to shake his hand and tell him their problems. On TV he set a precedent by echoing average citizens' complaints. Up until that time, no Soviet leader had ever so publicly criticized the communist system.

Gorbachev's first year in office was described by a Russian word meaning "economic reconstruction" or "rebuilding." That word—perestroika—was also defined as a "major transformation of the mind."[28] Perestroika ushered in another era in Soviet history, called glasnost, in which the government pledged more honesty, openness, less talk, and more action. Perestroika did not stop the downward spiral of the Soviet economy. "But glasnost, the new tolerance, helped change the world."[29] According to the Associated Press:

> Gorbachev realized that the Soviet economy, indeed the entire Soviet system, was a shambles. The Soviets could not feed their own peo-

ple, let alone successfully compete with the United States in a high-tech arms race.[30]

Gorbachev and Reagan Summits

When Mikhail Gorbachev came to power, Ronald Reagan wanted to meet him. "I have a gut feeling," the president wrote in his diary, "I'd like to talk to him about our problems man to man and see if I could convince him there would be a material benefit to the Soviets if they'd join the family of nations, etc."[31]

In November 1985, Reagan called for a "season of peace" with the Soviet Union and expressed high hopes for a summit meeting with Gorbachev. The two leaders met in Geneva, Switzerland, on November 19 and 20. Although the meeting produced little in the way of arms reduction, the two men spent hours away from handlers and advisers getting to know each other. Both leaders expressed optimism and agreed to meet again.

In October 1986, Gorbachev and Reagan renewed their face-to-face acquaintance, in Reykjavik, Iceland. They announced agreements on positions that had separated their respective sides for a generation. Significant progress was made on the issues of strategic and medium-range missiles, nuclear testing, and other aspects of

Star Wars

In 1983 Reagan went on national television and called for the deployment of a futuristic defense system that would destroy Soviet missiles in flight. The plan was called the Strategic Defense Initiative (SDI) but quickly became known as "Star Wars" after the George Lucas film. At the time of the speech, many of Reagan's closest advisers knew nothing about the plan, which existed more on paper than in fact. David Wright discusses Reagan's plan in *America in the 20th Century: 1980–1989*.

> "Star Wars" never got off the ground. In fact, it may have been an idea Ronald Reagan retrieved from a movie in which he had once starred. The idea was simple: Construct a high-tech, defensive umbrella that would knock out missiles aimed at the United States while they were still far out in space. This protection against ICBMs (intercontinental ballistic missiles) cost billions and would have taken years to construct and it called for technology not yet invented. Despite its science-fiction quality, Reagan and his advisors bristled when reporters labeled it "Star Wars."

Although many said that the Star Wars concept could not be realized in practice, being as unachievable as "shooting a bullet with another bullet," one important person thought it might work. Soviet leader Mikhail Gorbachev took the SDI threat seriously enough to sign several arms control pacts with the United States. More than $50 billion has been spent on the SDI program over the years, but there have been few positive results, and no such weapons system existed as of 1998.

arms control. But the talks broke down over a single issue: Star Wars and the Soviet fears that this U.S. policy initiative would result in a hazardous and expensive race in unpredictable new technology. When the talks broke down, Gorbachev asserted that the Soviets "are not really concerned about SDI. I think even in America no one believes that such a system can be developed." [32]

But Gorbachev walked out of the summit because he believed that the development of a defensive shield of laser weapons in space would open the door to deployment of offensive weapons. Gorbachev's advisers thought the proposed SDI relied too heavily on computers, which might malfunction. The Secretary General also acknowledged that launching a Soviet space weapons program to counter the U.S. system would mean a heavy financial drain on an already sluggish economy.

In July 1987 Gorbachev announced that the Soviets would eliminate their intermediate-range nuclear missiles if the United States would do the same. On December 8, Reagan and Gorbachev sat down in the White House to sign the historic agreement that would destroy

Ronald Reagan and Mikhail Gorbachev chat before the fire in Geneva, Switzerland, in 1985. Gorbachev endeared himself to the United States by publicly admitting that the Soviet system was flawed and by initiating talks to negotiate nuclear weapons reductions.

859 U.S. missiles along with 1,836 Soviet missiles within three years. It was the first pact between the two nations that actually eliminated nuclear weapons.

Reagan and Gorbachev held another meeting, this one in Moscow in May 1988. No new agreements on nuclear weapons were made, but Reagan used the trip to promote human rights and to show the world how remarkably American-Soviet relations had changed. Perhaps the most important proof of the change was Reagan's statement that he no longer thought of the Soviet Union as "an evil empire."

The Crack-Up of the Soviet Union

The concessions offered by the Soviets at the various summit meetings made Gorbachev very popular in the West.

Mikhail Gorbachev and Ronald Reagan sign the intermediate-range nuclear forces (INF) treaty at the White House in 1987. Gorbachev initiated arms reductions primarily because he knew the Soviets could not afford to keep producing the weapons.

But the general secretary knew that he had no choice. The Soviet Union was quickly falling apart and could not compete in a fantastically expensive arms race with the United States. By the time Gorbachev became the leader of the USSR, there were already cracks in the iron curtain. In 1980 workers in the shipyards of Gdansk, Poland, had gone on strike demanding a higher standard of living. Their leader, Lech Walesa, had become an international hero practi-

cally overnight. Ten million Polish workers had organized their trade unions into one movement called Solidarity, and the CIA had funneled secret funds to Poles to keep Solidarity alive. The movement had the important support of other workers, intellectuals, and the Catholic Church.

Soviet leaders had threatened to send in the army to quash Solidarity. But rather than risk an all-out war in Poland, a country of 37 million people, the Soviets ordered the Solidarity movement leaders arrested. On December 31, 1981, the Polish government ordered mass arrests of Solidarity members, including Walesa, as well as workers, scientists, scholars, writers, and artists. Public and private gatherings were banned. Martial law was declared.

But it was too late to stop Solidarity. The movement had spread like wildfire across Eastern Europe. Lech Walesa had been released from prison in 1982 and on June 5, 1989 he was elected president of Poland in that country's first democratic election in forty years. Five months later, the Berlin Wall came down. On December 10, the first non-

Lech Walesa (center), leader of the Polish Solidarity movement, was a driving force behind loosening the Soviet Union's grip on Poland. The movement ultimately succeeded, and Walesa was elected president in the first elections in Poland since before World War II.

communist government in forty-one years took power in Czechoslovakia. After a bloody revolt in Romania, communism fell there on December 27. By the first months of 1990, the Soviet Union itself was cracking up. The fifteen republics comprising the Union of Soviet Socialist Republics were demanding the same freedoms as the countries of Eastern Europe.

As the 1990s began, the Communist grip on Europe had melted away like the winter snows. On August 29, 1991, the Supreme Soviet legislature voted to suspend all activities of the Communist party. By Christmas, the Soviet Union had unraveled and was renamed the Commonwealth of Independent States. The Soviet regime passed into history at the age of seventy-four. The collapse was so swift and complete that many wondered why the Soviet Union had frightened them for so long.

Chapter Three

Traders on the New York Stock Exchange floor huddle during the panic selling spree of October 19, 1987. On what came to be known as "Black Monday," the Dow Jones average plunged over five hundred points.

Wall Street and Corporate Power

While the Soviet Union was lurching from one crisis to another, the United States was experiencing one of the largest economic booms in history. And the keyword in the eighties world of business was deregulation.

Companies large and small had tired of the paperwork and expense of complying with the ever-growing list of government-imposed rules and regulations. Many health and safety rules made sense, but there were so many regulations that businesses often found it difficult to comply with them all.

The 1960s and 1970s were decades in which more and more government regulations were applied to big corporations. During those decades, new bureaucracies were created within the federal government to protect citizens and the environment. The Environmental Protection Agency (EPA), the Consumer Products Safety Commission, and the Occupational Health and Safety Administration (OSHA) are three such agencies.

The early sixties saw many new federal regulations. For example, automakers were obliged to redesign their products to accommodate seat belts, shoulder harnesses, impact-absorbing bumpers, and pollution-reduction equipment. The Clean Air and Clean Water Acts imposed restrictions on pollution from steel mills, power plants, chemical refineries, and other factories whose waste disposal practices had been established in the nineteenth century or before.

From the beginning, corporations questioned the authority of the federal government to regulate their practices. They charged that regulations cost them billions of dollars to institute and when the cost was passed on to consumers, consumers complained. Industry opposition surfaced, for example, when the Clean Air and Clean Water Acts came up for review in the early 1980s. Businesses lobbied intensely on several issues in an effort to weaken the requirements imposed by the original legislation.

First, industry charged that EPA standards put an unreasonable curb on

When the federal government tried to curb industrial pollution with new environmental legislation, businesses fought it on the political front. Environmentalists wanted to end scenes such as this smokestack spewing pollutants into the air.

industrial expansion. Second, critics contended that the standards were too restrictive. One spokesman for the Business Roundtable summed up his organization's position: "Nobody wants to jeopardize the public health. But the question is, how clean is clean?"[33] In the third place, businesses wanted a cost-benefit analysis of every regulation—

they wanted lawmakers to determine what a proposed ruling would cost to implement versus the benefit to the public—before each such measure became law. The cost of pollution control and bureaucratic red tape were other issues of concern.

These businesses had a friend in Ronald Reagan. In his first full week in office, the president put a freeze on all new federal regulations—an action he had promised during his campaign. Reagan's regulation freeze directed the heads of the Environmental Protection Agency and all cabinet-level departments (except Defense) to delay new regulations and refrain from issuing new ones for sixty days.

Corporate Power and Government Regulation

While large corporations have always had a great deal of power in America, in the eighties, corporations grew even more powerful:

Many of today's massive corporations are larger than most nations in which they do business. Of the 213 nations on the earth, there are only seven—the United States, Japan, France, Germany, Italy, the United Kingdom, and Canada—that report gross national products (GNP) greater than

Air Traffic Controllers Strike

Ronald Reagan was once head of the Screen Actors Guild, a powerful Hollywood union. But by the time he was elected president, Reagan's attitude toward organized labor had changed. On August 3, 1981, the 11,600 member Professional Air Traffic Controllers Organization (PATCO) went on strike. The air traffic controllers were responsible for directing takeoffs, landings, and routings at all commercial airports in the United States. The strike was illegal: the union had pledged never to violate public safety by going on strike. When the controllers failed to report for work, the nation's commercial air traffic was grounded.

Although three years of training is needed to produce a skilled controller, Reagan fired all the strikers on August 5. According to Associated Press news reports, the president said, "What lesser action can there be? The law is very specific and they are violating the law." The president's decisive action was overwhelmingly supported by the business community. The PATCO workers were not rehired, although some came back to work after dropping their union membership. As the decade progressed, tough anti-union stances were assumed by many businesses, and union power declined significantly in America.

the assets of the world's leading banks. General Motors had revenues greater than the gross national products of 191 (or 89.7%) of all the world's nations.[34]

Corporate operations vitally influence the lives of every American citizen. In 1988 the top one hundred companies in the Fortune 500 employed over two-thirds of all workers engaged in manufacturing, controlled two-thirds of all industrial sales, and earned four-fifths of all corporate profits. Their combined assets reached $2 trillion, and their total profits in 1988 were $115 billion.

General Motors, one of the largest industrial corporations in the world, made $121 billion in sales in 1988. Its expenditures ranked it seventh among all the countries in the world. Other giants like AT&T, Philip Morris, Ford, IBM, Exxon, and General Electric continued to grow through mergers and acquisitions. And a few firms dominated entire markets—GM produced practically all diesel locomotives; Western Electric produced virtually all telephone equipment; Campbell's Foods sold 95 percent of the prepared soup in America. This type of market concentration is known as oligopoly from the Greek words meaning "few sellers."

The business recovery of the eighties was due partly to the Reagan ad-ministration's relaxation of regulations on large corporations. The auto industry did not hesitate to make known the regulations it found burdensome. On August 18, 1981, the *Wall Street Journal* reported:

> Most of all, the automakers want to substantively roll back certain car and truck pollution rules, completely revamp emissions enforcement, junk a requirement for automobile crash protection devices for passengers, and dilute existing standards for bumpers.[35]

Other industries were after deregulation as well. The Reagan administration rolled back or cut enforcement on thousands of regulations in the areas of medical drugs, air and water pollution, toxic chemicals, and car design and engineering.

Merger Mania

Besides industrial corporations, the Reagan administration eased restrictions on the stock market and other financial institutions. Antitrust laws—statutes designed to prevent concentration of economic power in a few very powerful firms—were not enforced rigorously in the 1980s. In a reversal from its traditional role, the Securities and Exchange Commission (SEC), the agency that regulates financial markets, took what many interpreted as a favorable view on stock speculation. This began a wave of corporate takeovers unimaginable in earlier years—a wave that continues to this day.

Some of the largest corporate takeovers in history happened in the eighties. More than half the nation's thousand largest companies underwent some sort of restructuring or merger. In all, more than twenty-five thousand mergers or takeovers occurred. Corporate giants swallowed up or took over retail stores, oil companies, and anything else that made a profit. The biggest merger of all was between R. J. Reynolds, the tobacco company, and Nabisco, maker of cookies, crackers, and cereals. The deal totaled $24.9 billion.

Other companies were taken over in what is called a leveraged buyout, in which investors join forces with the managers of a company to buy that company. The participants usually form a private, separate company for this purpose. The funds come partly from the managers themselves, and some are borrowed. In a

Businessmen go into work with little fanfare after their company, R. J. Reynolds, merged with Nabisco in one of the largest mergers ever.

leveraged buyout, the assets of the company that is being acquired are used to guarantee the loans necessary to make the buyout.

During the 1980s, companies with very low debt loads were attractive targets for leveraged buyouts by speculators known as "corporate raiders." The companies that had been bought out were saddled with huge debts, which often could be repaid only by laying off workers and selling assets. Sometimes, to prevent these unwanted effects of hostile takeovers, recently acquired companies bought back their stock at prices much higher than market value—in effect, paying the raiders to go away. This practice became known as "greenmail," for its resemblance to blackmail, except that it was not illegal.

For example, in 1984 Walt Disney Productions faced a takeover threat from financier Saul Steinberg, who owned 11 percent of the company's stock. Disney bought back its stock, valued at $50 a share, for $70. More than $2 billion in greenmail was paid by corporations such as Texaco, Warner, and Quaker State in the first few months of 1984.

Yuppies

Each business merger requires armies of brokers, lawyers, and bankers. In the 1980s, this created a whole new class of business people known as "young, urban professionals," or yuppies. More often than not the term applied to white men and women between college age and forty. They dressed well, lived in expensive apartments, drove expensive cars (especially BMWs), worked out in gyms, and worked all day in banking, law, or high-tech management jobs.

David Wright describes yuppies of the 1980s in his book *America in the 20th Century: 1980–1989.*

People saw money as power. Young executives consumed "power lunches" while wearing fashionable "power suits." Labels crept from the inside to the outside of clothes, as designer fashions boosted egos and fattened the cash registers of swank stores. The trend broadened as everything from t-shirts to blue jeans to tennis shoes sported distinctive logos—the swoosh of Nike, the red tab of Levi Strauss, and the intricate initialing of Chanel.

[Yuppies] annoyed the rest of the population in different ways. Older and less affluent Americans considered them ostentatious. Cars such as BMWs became symbols of excess to people who were trying to patch together aging Chevys or Fords. On college campuses, "Die yuppie scum!" became a popular bumper sticker. But there were many collegians eagerly awaiting their chance to become urban professionals too.

A total of $1.3 trillion was spent on corporate acquisitions in the 1980s. That sum was roughly equal to the entire annual output of West Germany in those years. Merger mania and corporate takeovers did not happen in America alone. Japanese corporations alone had $18 trillion at their disposal for buying business assets, including American companies and real estate.

Merger mania had its downside as well. Thousands of workers lost their jobs, companies assumed crushing loads of debt to pay for deals, profits were sacrificed to pay interest costs on loans, and bankruptcies rose to record levels. Sometimes bondholders and shareholders lost millions.

Junk Bonds

The money for many takeovers was raised by the sale of so-called junk bonds. Junk bonds are classified as high-risk investments by securities rating agencies, such as Standard & Poor's and Moody's; they are more likely than higher rated bonds not to be repaid. The people who issue junk bonds tend not to have long track records, or their credit may be shaky. These bonds are also called high-yield bonds since along with the higher risk goes the potential for higher yield. That is, if a takeover is successful, people who bought its bonds—the "junk" bonds—

are handsomely rewarded, often out of profits made from selling off pieces of the company taken over.

Junk bonds, mergers, and acquisitions first became the watchwords of investors in the 1980s. But the roots of the takeover boom were probably as much psychological as financial. Many explanations have been offered for the sudden, almost frenzied effort to buy existing companies rather than create new ones. In his book *Den of Thieves,* about junk bond kings and corporate raiders who operated outside the law, *Wall Street Journal* reporter James B. Stewart writes about the buying frenzy of the 1980s.

The election of Ronald Reagan in 1980 sent a powerful "anything goes" message to the financial markets. Bigness apparently wasn't going to be a problem in the new era of unbridled capitalism. Suddenly, economics of scale could be realized in already oligopolistic industries such as oil, where mergers wouldn't even have been considered in the Carter years.

What really fueled the boom was the sight of other people making money, big money, by buying companies and selling them. When the former secretary of the treasury (under Nixon and Ford) William Simon bought Gibson Greetings in

1982 and then resold it sixteen months later at a profit of $70 million, Wall Street couldn't stop talking [about the huge profits made by Simon]. Corporate raiders began to emerge realizing that just about anybody could buy a company, slash expenses or break off prices ruthlessly, and then unload the assets at a huge gain. The next best thing to buying and selling companies, and much less risky, was to be the investment banker [or] lawyer . . . standing by as money changed hands.[36]

A few successful corporate raiders operated outside the law. It has always been illegal to play the market assisted by information not available to average investors. This is called "insider trading." One of the simplest forms of insider trading occurs when a person initiating a corporate takeover tells colleagues to buy as much stock as possible in the company before the general public finds out about the deal. When the announcement is made that the company is to be sold, the stock price often rises quickly. Those who bought the stock ahead of the official statement reap large profits, which they are expected to share with the insider.

There are other, more complicated ways to take advantage of insider trading, and they are illegal, as well. The first big insider trading arrest of the decade was on May 12, 1986. Dennis Levine had made $12.6 million on insider-trading deals. He worked for the powerhouse junk-bond firm Drexel Burnham Lambert Inc. After Levine was arrested, he implicated two well-known Wall Street traders, Michael Milken, also of Drexel, and independent arbitrageur Ivan Boesky (a special-

Ivan Boesky pled guilty to criminal charges brought against him for insider trading. Boesky was fined $100 million.

Michael Milken

Financier Michael R. Milken first learned about "junk bonds" when he joined the firm of Drexel Burnham Lambert. At the time most brokerage houses ignored these securities because even though they often performed well, they were not considered to be investment quality. Milken, however, began selling junk bonds aggressively. By the early 1980s, he was reportedly making $550 million a year. In 1986 Milken became the target of a federal fraud investigation based on his dealings with financier turned government informant Ivan Boesky.

Milken eventually pleaded guilty, paid fines of $1.1 billion, and served twenty-two months in jail (and Drexel collapsed). He insists that junk bonds "change[d] the flow of capital to those people that had ability rather than those people who were born with money." Indeed, junk bonds helped make possible rapid growth and job creation at such enterprises as MCI Communications and Turner Broadcasting. On the day he was released from prison in March 1993,

Michael Milken smiles at supporters while leaving federal court in 1989.

Milken learned that he had prostate cancer; he pledged $25 million of his still considerable personal fortune to fund research on the disease.

ist in rapid purchases and resales of stocks or currency). Both men were charged with many violations of federal securities laws—in effect, insider trading. After his arrest, Boesky agreed to pay $100 million in forfeitures and penalties—a fraction of his illegal gains over the years. Michael Milken's crimes were complex, imaginative, and ambitious and went beyond mere insider trading. In just one year, 1986, Milken earned over $500 million in salary and bonus. He admitted to six felonies and agreed to pay $600 million in fines, an amount larger than the entire yearly budget of the SEC.

Black Monday

Throughout the eighties, the volume of shares traded on the nation's stock markets continued to grow. The Dow Jones Industrial Average, a measure of the market as represented by the New York Stock Exchange, started the decade at 1,100 points. By autumn of 1987, that worth had more than doubled to 2,500 points. In the first eight months of 1987, the market hit record highs fifty-five times. Several economists warned of a crash, but the public paid little heed. In October 1987, markets in Asia and Europe went on the skids. This frightened investors, who started selling their stocks. On October 19, or Black Monday, the stock market went into free fall.

Many stock-buying services used computers that automatically sold chunks of stock when the Dow Jones average began to fall. As the volume of sales by nervous investors mounted, the programmed selling accelerated accordingly. Soon computers all over Wall Street were selling stock at blinding speed, causing a panic. Before it was over, the market fell a record (for that time)

Traders populate the floor of the New York Stock Exchange as the Dow Jones plunges a record 508 points on Black Monday.

508 points. That represented a loss of $500 billion, the equivalent of the en-

tire gross national product of France.

That loss came out of the pockets of investors big and small, but one-third of those who lost money were small investors. The free fall spelled disaster for fundamental American institutions. Brokerage houses could not keep up with the paperwork and financial demands. The entire financial system faced collapse. The Federal Reserve Board, the nation's central bank, came to the rescue by pumping millions of dollars into the system to keep it functioning.

The market finally stopped its downward spiral and began a rally for the next few days. Once the market turned around, people tried to determine why it had crashed. Some blamed an interest rate hike in West Germany. Others blamed a bill in Congress that would have made mergers and acquisi-

A trader frantically tries to sell the stock he is holding. Black Monday caused widespread panic among investors and the general public.

tions more difficult. Others simply credited investor jitters in the big sell-off. Later, changes were made to prevent computers from automatically dumping huge chunks of stock and risking another panic.

The Savings and Loan Debacle

Lack of government regulation was also found in the banking industry. In 1982 Republican senator Jake Garn of Utah and Democratic congressman Ferdinand St. Germain of Louisiana wrote a bill that would change the way the nation's savings and loan (S&L) banks operated. On October 15, 1982, the Garn–St. Germain bill was signed by Ronald Reagan, who said, "All in all, I think we hit the jackpot."[37] With the stroke of a pen, Reagan freed the nation's S&Ls from restrictive federal regulations and gave them permission to expand beyond their traditional role of making home and car loans.

Savings and loans are sometimes called "thrift institutions" to distinguish them from commercial banks which issue credit cards and lend mostly to businesses. In the early 1980s, S&Ls obtained the bulk of their funds from consumer savings accounts. The S&Ls lent this money to average citizens for car loans and home mortgages.

Thrift institutions operated under strict laws made during the Great Depression of the 1930s when seventeen hundred savings banks went bankrupt, wiping out the savings of people who had no other funds. The regulations limited the amount of interest a bank could pay on a savings account and restricted S&Ls from offering checking accounts. In return, the government guaranteed each account; that is, if an S&L failed, its depositors would eventually receive at least some of their savings from federal funds.

Interest rates in the 1970s were unusually high and many consumers pulled their money from low-interest accounts in S&Ls to take advantage of the higher yields available from Treasury bills and money market funds. Thus many S&Ls, which had the bulk of their money invested in long-term, low-interest mortgages, were forced to go out of business.

When Congress passed the Garn–St. Germain bill, it was to help the S&Ls by phasing out interest-rate ceilings. S&Ls also were allowed to take on higher yielding (and high-risk) investments; and long-standing safeguards—such as the requirement that S&Ls have multiple shareholders to prevent any one owner from "milking" the profits—were abandoned. Federal supervision was limited as well, and accounting rules were relaxed, which allowed troubled S&Ls to conceal their insolvency. Whereas depositors' accounts had been insured for a maximum of $40,000, the 1982 bill raised that amount to $100,000.

Because depositors' accounts were insured by the government, thrift operators had little reason to act prudently in planning their investments that often focused on risky ventures. "It was a phenomenon economists call the moral hazard: If an S&L's gambles paid off, its owners won big," says author Kathleen Day. "If it lost the gambles, the taxpayers picked up the tab."[38] This new banking environment was a bonanza for many high rollers, get-rich-quick artists, and swindlers.

Many analysts blame Ronald Reagan's probusiness, antiregulation policies for some of the economic problems that plagued the 1980s, including the savings and loan crisis.

Insiders Reap Profits

Soon the S&Ls were offering up to 13 percent interest rates, which attracted many new customers. The new money poured out of the thrifts into speculative investments in real estate, condominiums, oil and gas ventures, and high-yielding junk bonds. Some bank presidents and industry insiders reaped huge profits in a short time. They bought luxurious estates, fine artwork, airplanes, and yachts with the deposits.

The entire S&L structure collapsed in a shakeout of the real estate and financial markets in the late 1980s. Between 1980 and 1990, more than twelve hundred savings institutions experienced troubles that were severe enough to require federal assistance. Fraud was discovered in 60 percent of the failed thrifts. Depositors learned that their money had been invested in worthless buildings and land, or in junk bonds, or had been stolen outright. "Reports of Mafia influence and CIA money laundering operations circulated and the taxpayer was the guarantor of deposits resulting from drug trafficking."[39]

The savings and loan collapse became one of the greatest financial scandals in American history. Ultimately, since much of the money lost from federally guaranteed accounts had to be repaid to the original depositors, taxpayers wound up financing the bailout of the failed S&Ls. If the bailout had occurred in 1984, it would have cost about $40 billion. In 1990, however, the price tag had grown to $500 billion, or $2,000 for every man, woman, and child in America. Yet most Americans failed to appreciate the magnitude of the scandal.

Robbing Their Own Banks

Very few people went to jail for illegal activities that could be described as S&L fraud. Both Democrats and Republicans had supported the bill to deregulate the thrifts. The looming S&L crisis was a nonissue in the 1988 presidential race between George Bush and Massachusetts governor Michael Dukakis. After the election, the bills came due, and Congress was forced to set aside billions of dollars to clean up the S&L mess. California thrift commissioner William Crawford summed up the situation when he said: "The best way to rob a bank is to own one."[40]

The End of the Go-Go Decade

While the eighties are remembered as the go-go decade, the country entered a deep recession around July 1990 which continued until 1992. During this recession unemployment rose from 5.2 percent to 7.8 percent as businesses turned to repaying the debts incurred during the eighties. Companies laid off workers and "downsized" their operations. A massive scale-back in defense contracts forced the layoff of thousands of workers in the defense industry.

Many people got rich in the 1980s, but the era had its critics. Studies showed that the gulf between rich and poor grew wider. As Kevin Phillips, an assistant attorney general in the Nixon administration, writes:

The 1980s were a triumph of upper America—an ostentatious celebration of wealth, the political ascendancy of the richest third of the population and a glorification of capitalism, free markets, and finance. But while money, greed, and luxury had become the stuff of popular culture, hardly anyone asked why such great wealth had concentrated at the top, and whether this was the result of public policy. Despite the armies of homeless sleeping on grates, political leaders had little to say about the Republican party's historical role, which has been not simply to revitalize U.S. capitalism but to tilt power, policy, wealth, and income towards the richest portions of the population.[41]

Whatever the case, the 1980s will be remembered as an era of high-flying mergers, frenzied investment, corporate raiders, S&L collapse, and a roller-coaster stock market.

Chapter Four

Farmers stage a protest at the Chicago Mercantile exchange in January 1985. A steep decline in land and produce prices forced many farmers to sell their holdings when the value of their harvests was insufficient to cover their annual expenses.

Lives of Everyday People

During the 1980s, studies showed that the wealthiest Americans were getting richer, while poor Americans fell behind. "Average family income for those in the poorest fifth of the population declined by 6.1 percent from 1979 to 1987, while family income for the highest paid Americans rose by 11.1 percent during this same period."[42] The loss of 1.6 million man-ufacturing jobs in the blue collar job market was one of the reasons for this decline.

Until the double shock of rising energy prices and inflation increased the cost of living in the 1970s, many Americans had been able to find jobs that provided a comfortable living. Along the Great Lakes and throughout the Midwest, unionized factory workers held jobs that paid decent wages and offered health and retirement benefits. The strengths of the steel, chemical, and automobile industries held up a middle-class standard of living for tens of millions of Americans. But that changed radically in the late seventies and early eighties when modern German and Asian steel mills and industrial plants drove many antiquated American factories out of business.

Far from Wall Street's vision of supply-side riches, a feeling of failure gripped America's industrial heartland. Across Pennsylvania, Ohio, and Indiana, across Michigan and up into the Iron Range of Minnesota, factories were shuttered, their smokestacks crumbling. What was once America's Steel Belt became known as the Rust Belt.

Signs of collapse were everywhere in the region. Roads and bridges were closed because declining tax bases left no money for states to repair them. Stores along the main streets of small towns were boarded up. Downtown areas in Detroit, in Youngstown, Ohio, and in other industrial cities became ghost towns. One popular bumper sticker read: "Last one out of Cleveland—Turn out the lights." Cars, campers, trucks, and motorcycles carried "For Sale" signs. Unemployment rates were stuck in double-digit figures.

As Pulitzer Prize–winning author Haynes Johnson writes:

In industrial community after community, a familiar pathology of poverty emerged. Social agencies reported an increase in family abuse cases, in drinking and drug use, acts of violence, and divorce. Older people became increasingly fearful of losing their Social Security benefits after hearing horror stories of others being cut from the rolls.

Management and labor blamed each other for outmoded union work rules and for placing desire for profits over welfare of employees, and both blamed the government. Everyone blamed foreigners.[43]

The plight of the Rust Belt symbolized what was happening to many areas of U.S. society: as the industrial base eroded, more people became displaced, creating more of a gap between the richest citizens and the poorest.

Statistics released by the U.S. Census Bureau showed this growing divide. For instance, in 1975, the poorest 5 percent of Americans earned an average of $5,000 a year. The top 5 percent earned an average of $90,000. By 1985, the income of the poorest 5 percent remained about the same, while the top 5 percent had shot up to

A mother and her children sit on the porch of their home in an impoverished Detroit neighborhood. As unemployment climbed, more people found themselves in desperate circumstances.

an average of $120,000 a year. Meanwhile, those in the middle saw their average incomes grow from about $35,000 a year to only $40,000.

In 1983 a Department of Labor report stated that at least 20 percent of all factory workers had been unemployed for at least part of the past twelve months. Numbers from the Bureau of Labor Statistics show that between 1981 and 1987, America lost about 400,000 jobs in the machinery industry, 235,000 jobs in the steel industry, and 200,000 jobs in the oil, gas, and mining industry. Manufacturing, overall, lost over a million jobs.

While heavy industry was declining, many jobs were created in the lower-paying service industries. Three million new jobs were created in the retail trade and about 1 million in the food and drink industry. The building boom helped create about 700,000 jobs in the construction industry. And the hot financial markets created about 1.3 million jobs in finance, insurance, and real estate.

People who were forced from industrial jobs into the service sector became known as the working poor. But factory workers were not the only ones who were suffering. By 1988, the American dream was imperiled for many segments of society. In *The Politics of Rich and Poor,* Kevin Phillips writes of the general feelings of some Americans:

The average wage seemed to buy less. Low-income households were in trouble, especially female-headed ones. Here and there, off main roads, large patches of small-town America were dying. Big-city poverty was on the rise. Young married couples, needing two incomes to meet bills, postponed having children and gave up buy-ing their own homes. And in blue-collar factory towns, where a job on the production line at Ford or Bethlehem Steel had helped two generations of workers climb into the middle class, the next generation saw no such opportunity.[44]

Population Shift to the South and West

While the Rust Belt was floundering in the late 1970s, the Sun Belt was booming. This caused a massive shift in America's population centers during the 1980s. A steady stream of people flowed out of the northeast and north-central states into the southern and western regions. Between 1978 and 1981 alone, over 3 million people moved to the South and 400,000 migrated to the West.

The entire Sun Belt was prospering, but the development of the "oil patch" in Texas, west of Houston, led the way. This was due in part to the unprecedented jump in oil prices during the 1970s. The president of Pennzoil summarized the oil boom when he said:

Why the rest of the country could be having a depression, but you don't know it down here [in Houston]. I used to live in Pittsburgh, and God, we went through some of those recessions up there. People in the alleys, you know. Burning stuff

The Fall of the Family Farm

Until the 1980s America's farmers had been enjoying boom times. Long years of inflation caused a corresponding increase in the price of farmland. In the Midwest in the 1970s, the average price of farmland rose from $193 an acre to $725. As the price of land kept rising, farmers went on a spending spree, borrowing money against the inflated value of their land. More and more heavy equipment was bought, more outbuildings and animals were purchased, and major home improvements were made.

Farmers and their families gather at the Capitol in Washington, D.C., to lobby for federal price supports for crops and to stop farm foreclosures. Economic conditions in the 1980s severely harmed farmers.

Then in the mid-1980s, the bottom fell out of land prices *and* food prices. In Minnesota alone, land prices plummeted from $1,947 an acre to $628 an acre, wiping out $30 billion of the net worth of Minnesota farmers. Across the Farm Belt there was a rash of bankruptcies, forced auctions, and foreclosures; also very much in evidence were falling land values, lower commodity prices, lack of cash flow, and production surpluses. It was the biggest agricultural shakeout since the Great Depression of the 1930s.

The U.S. farm population dropped from 9 million in 1975 to 5 million in 1987. As agribusiness companies bought up family farms, thousands of farmhouses were torn down and plowed under. Interviews with families forced out of farming showed high incidence of withdrawal from friends and family, depression, feelings of worthlessness, mood swings, and increased physical aggressiveness. Researchers also found high levels of frequent illness, headaches, fatigue, forgetfulness, loss of temper, lack of concentration, back pain, sleep disruptions, behavioral problems in children, and marriage problems.

in the barrel. You came down here to Houston—they didn't even know it was happening.[45]

(A few years later, Texas would learn about recessions when oil prices fell and the real estate market bottomed out.)

Farther west, in California, a new kind of America was being born forty miles south of San Francisco. In 1980 Silicon Valley held the promise of a prosperous successful new America. The technology of computers had created new fortunes and new communities to support them. The computer boom was said to be recession proof and pollution free.

The heart of Silicon Valley is Sunnyvale, California. Lured by stories of new success, the nation's brightest engineers began moving there along with risk takers, pioneers, venture capitalists, and other creators of eighties economic legend. While the Rust Belt suffered through the changing economy, people in northern California showed that the American economy could be flexible and that change could be positive. According to Haynes Johnson:

Elsewhere Americans might think that the country has lost its way or that the government had broken down, or fear the country was in decline, or despair of the future.

For the people of Silicon Valley, there was no such pessimism. Their vision was Reagan's vision, and the country hungered for it. It was a vision of success.[46]

Women in the Eighties

Women continued to make gains in the 1980s. In 1981 the Supreme Court ruled that a woman could sue her employer over "comparable worth." This meant that a woman who did the same kind of work as a man should be paid the same wages as a man. While the ruling did not immediately bring about equal pay for equal work, there was an improvement. Department of Labor statistics show that in 1979 a woman made sixty two cents for every dollar earned by a man. By 1987 it was seventy cents for every dollar. But one economist pointed out that the gain was relative because the average wage for men had actually gone down.

Statistics aside, women went to work in the 1980s in unprecedented numbers as economics required two breadwinners in a household to pay for home mortgages, new cars, clothing, and other desired items.

Divorce continued to rise during the decade as it had for years. In the 1970s, single-parent families, mostly with a female head, made up 13 percent of the total. In 1980, the number of single-parent families jumped to 22 percent. By 1987, that number was 27 percent. A study by economist Lauri Bassi showed that divorce was often forcing previously nonworking females into minimum-wage jobs. Between 1980 and 1986 the inflation-adjusted income of female-headed households grew by only 2 percent while that of married couples grew by 9 percent.

Disturbing Trends for Children

Drugs, divorce, and family displacement had a growing effect on children during the 1980s. The number of

While some sectors of the economy were suffering in the 1980s, high-tech fields dealing with computer development, programming, and technology were booming.

Women Making Headlines

During the 1980 campaign, Ronald Reagan promised to name a woman to fill one of the first Supreme Court vacancies of his administration. When Justice Potter Stewart retired in 1981, the president nominated an Arizona judge, Sandra Day O'Connor, as the first woman justice in the 191 years of the Supreme Court. Reagan called it the "most awesome appointment" within his power.

In the other political camp, Democrats made history in 1984 when presidential candidate Walter Mondale selected New York congresswoman Geraldine Ferraro as his running mate. Ferraro became the first woman to be on a major party's ticket for national office. "Housewives and hardened professionals alike felt a new dignity," according to Associated Press writer William A. Henry, "a new belief that the system can work for them, too. The mantle of honor would rest on just one woman. But every woman in America

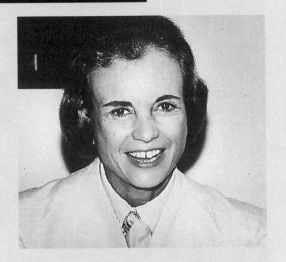

Sandra Day O'Connor, the first female Supreme Court justice, was appointed by Ronald Reagan.

who had spoken up for equality could feel that her effort in some way had helped."

Americans living in poverty increased from under 10 percent in 1978 to over 14 percent—or 33 million people—by 1988. One of every four Americans living in poverty was a child—a total of 8.25 million people. The nation's infant mortality rate grew until it was higher than that of seventeen other industrial nations. A child born in the United States was between two and three times as likely to be poor as one born in Germany, Sweden, Norway, or Canada. The numbers were worse among mi-

norities. By 1989 the government reported that half of all African-American children were living in poverty.

Poverty, family breakdown, and other troubles magnified problems emanating from America's public schools. In 1983 a federal study by the National Commission for Excellence in Education issued a report called "A Nation at Risk: The Imperative for Educational Reform." The study concluded that failure to improve education and schools would

This child's playground consists of the junked automobiles found in the scrap yard outside his home. Poverty often interferes with a child's ability to learn in school.

threaten the very foundations of the country. As David Wright notes:

Compared to children in other countries, Americans had inferior skills, and those skills were getting worse. Research showed that scores on college admissions tests had declined steadily for twenty years and that 13 percent of all seventeen-year-old American high school students were functionally illiterate.[47]

The study recommended that high schools require students to study English, mathematics, science, social studies, and computer studies, with special emphasis on foreign languages. It also called for the school year to increase from 180 days to 220 days a year and for teachers' pay to be based on merit.

Meanwhile, the dropout rate for high school students reached 26.7 percent and was higher in some areas.

Among eighteen- and nineteen-year-olds surveyed in 1987, only 77 percent of whites, 65 percent of blacks, and 55 percent of Hispanics had completed high school. Haynes Johnson wrote that "each year half a million teenagers dropped out of school to take menial, low-paying jobs, drift into unproductive idleness, or fall into the brutal world of the streets."[48]

The Homeless

The 1980s saw a large increase in the number of homeless people. Many of the homeless were families, others were former mental patients with no money and few prospects of employment who had been released from institutions. Some of the homeless were Vietnam veterans. Some held jobs but earned too little to pay for a room to live in.

The causes of homelessness included the rise of drug abuse, the shrinking number of rental properties, and a sharp rise in rent prices. Another root cause of homelessness was the withdrawal of the federal government from low-income housing programs, an effect of domestic budget cuts enacted during the Reagan administration. Many cities "gentrified" their central districts, replacing inexpensive, worn-out apartment buildings with high-rent properties and condominiums.

The problem was not confined to big cities. Kevin Phillips writes in *The Politics of Rich and Poor:*

Fifty years after [the depression] families were again bundling into cars and leaving behind farm foreclosures in Illinois, oil-field layoffs in Oklahoma, and closed mines in Minnesota. Bill Faith of the Ohio Coalition for the Homeless said, "Rural homelessness is growing faster than we can keep track of it. People are living

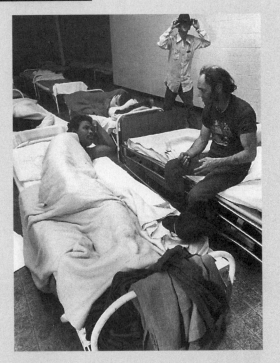

Homeless men find a safe haven from the elements in a Salvation Army shelter in Houston. Although the number of homeless was increasing, statistics widely varied on their exact number.

in railroad cars and tarpaper shacks. Shelters in tiny towns we've never heard of are operating at or above capacity and turning people away."

By the summer of 1988, 45.3 percent of New York City residents over the age of sixteen could not be counted on to function in the labor force. Author Kevin Phillips cites several reasons: "poverty, lack of skills, drug use, apathy, or other problems. Thus the paradox: millions of jobs might be going begging, but huge numbers of [young] Americans remained either unemployed or unemployable."[49]

Guns, Drugs, and Gangs

The 1980s had its share of crime and violence as well. An annual murder rate of more than twenty thousand was by far the world's highest, and half those deaths were the result of gunshot wounds. The number of guns in public possession continued to rise, approaching 100 million in a nation of 227 million people.

Law enforcement officials blamed the rise in crime on the flood of cocaine that was suddenly available on America's streets. Coke was smuggled into the country by Colombian drug cartels in an enterprise with estimated earnings of about $8 billion a year.

Powder cocaine was bad, but rock, or crack cocaine, was worse. Crack, a cheap form of cocaine, is often smoked by users looking for a very intense, instant high. The craving for crack is one of the strongest addictions known to humankind.

In the early eighties, before crack was introduced, about 6 million Americans were using cocaine. After crack became available, that number jumped to at least 10 million. Several high-profile celebrity deaths, followed by intense media coverage, put the drug issue on America's front pages.

Although the calamity of drug abuse was associated with the inner city, it reached into every class and community. One 1980s drug abuser was actor-comedian John Belushi, well known for his roles in *Animal House* and on *Saturday Night Live*. He was rich, he was famous, and he was strung out on heroin and cocaine. Belushi died from a drug overdose in 1982, at the age of thirty-three.

The drug issue jumped back on the front pages again in 1986.

Len Bias, a University of Maryland basketball star, celebrated being drafted by the Boston Celtics on June 19, 1986, by getting high. He died of a heart attack caused by [powder] cocaine. Eight days later, Don Rogers, a professional football player with the Cleveland Browns, took cocaine shortly before his wedding and died almost immediately. The two athletes became symbols, and important ones: if cocaine could kill even the most fit, who was safe from its effects?[50]

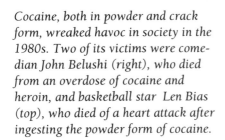

Cocaine, both in powder and crack form, wreaked havoc in society in the 1980s. Two of its victims were comedian John Belushi (right), who died from an overdose of cocaine and heroin, and basketball star Len Bias (top), who died of a heart attack after ingesting the powder form of cocaine.

When crack hit the inner cities, the landscape changed rapidly. Because people who are arrested before the age of eighteen generally escape long prison sentences, children and teenagers were put to work as lookouts and drug runners by dealers. Abandoned houses were suddenly inhabited by crack sellers. Desperate junkies lurked outside waiting for their next rock. Thousands of lives were destroyed as crack turned people into addicts virtually overnight.

Violence, theft, and murder increased dramatically where crack was found. Gangs, which had been in decline for decades, were suddenly growing in number as young organized criminals took control of the crack trade. There had always been street gangs in big cities such as New York, Cleveland, Los Angeles, and Chicago. When gangs reemerged in Los Angeles in the 1980s, authorities were not surprised.

Many gang members were addicted to crack, and their lack of self-control added a new element to the violence. Those who failed to flash the proper gang sign, for example, might be murdered in cold blood. There were gang-bangers of every race. They were male and female. They used their drug money to expand their power and buy fancy cars and more guns. Sometimes they were better armed than the police. Drive-by shootings, which killed as many innocent bystanders as rival gang members, became familiar tragedies in many poor neighborhoods.

The Los Angeles gangs began to branch out to Phoenix, San Francisco, Portland, Denver, and Kansas City. Once a gang established a foothold, drugs and guns flowed into the terri-

Officers stop a suspected gang member in Los Angeles, California. Gangs became more prevalent in the inner city, and their activities, usually centering on drugs and violence, threatened many neighborhoods.

Expanding U.S. Prison Population

In 1986 Congress passed legislation requiring harsh punishment for drug dealers. It created mandatory minimum sentences of five years for the sale of five grams of crack or five hundred grams of powdered cocaine.

Enforcement of the new drug laws resulted in an unprecedented rise in the number of prisoners in the United States. In 1980 there were about 5,000 federal drug prisoners. That number shot to 25,000 by 1990. Since state laws were also tightened, America held over 200,000 drug prisoners in state and federal penitentiaries. (By May 1998 that number leapt to 360,500.) As a result, the United States held more people in prison (per capita) than any nation in the world except the former Soviet Union, China, Iraq, and several other totalitarian regimes.

But as William Greider reports in the April 16, 1998, issue of *Rolling Stone* magazine:

Rand, the conservative think tank, calculated that every $1 million spent on extended sentences will reduce cocaine consumption by a modest 13 kilos. The same money spent treating drug addicts would reduce usage by 100 kilos.

In spite of the many alarms, cocaine is low on the list of killers. According to a 1988 report by the National Institute on Drug Abuse, tobacco killed 346,000 Americans and alcohol killed 125,000, followed by heroin or morphine which killed 4,000. Cocaine killed about 2,000 people that year, although crack's devastation to families and neighborhoods touched many more lives.

tory. Kids of all races began to dress and act like gangsters. They dressed in sports logos, wore bandannas, and flashed gang signs. Gangsta rap songs blared from cassette recorders across the country.

Gangs, guns, and drugs devastated the lives of thousands of families along with many who were simply in the wrong place at the wrong time. It was a problem that grew to unprecedented proportions in the 1980s, permanently changing the landscape and attitudes of America.

The Changing World

The decade of the eighties was a time of many drastic changes. The economic troubles of the seventies continued to damage lives and livelihoods well past 1980. America's great manufacturing base continued to decline.

Fortunately, Americans are a resilient people. New ways of living and new businesses replaced the old. As with every change, there were winners and there were losers. But America was no less a prosperous place in 1990 that it had been in 1980.

Chapter Five

Rock star Prince performs during the 1985 American Music Awards. A pop sensation in the eighties, Prince received numerous awards and accolades for his often controversial work.

Pop Culture: Off the Wall

The baby boomers, born between 1945 and 1965, left the world a legacy of rock and roll, the psychedelic sixties, and the yuppie excesses of the eighties. By 1980, many of the boomers were parents themselves. And it was their children who were dictating tastes in clothes, music, television, movies, and the arts. Some people called this generation "baby busters,"

others called them "Generation X." Whatever they were called, young people growing up in the eighties had an outlook markedly different from that of their parents, who were raised in the era of Vietnam and Flower Power. In describing the "Gen-Xers," Neil Howe and Bill Strauss explain:

When they were born, they were the first babies people took [birth control] pills not to have. When the 1967 Summer of Love marked the start of America's divorce epidemic, they were the wee kindergartners armed with latchkeys for re-entering empty homes after school. In 1974, they were the bell-bottomed seventh-graders who got their first real-life civics lesson watching Nixon resign on TV. Through the late 1970s, they were the teenage mallhoppers who spawned the "Valley Girls" and other flagrantly non-Boom youth trends. In 1979, they were the graduating seniors of Carter-era malaise who registered record low SAT scores and record high crime and drug-abuse rates.[51]

But while the younger generation was coming into its own, the huge population of baby boomers held the reins of power in the media. Baby boomers were the radio and television programmers, the record producers, and the moviemakers. This caused a rebellion fed by punk, new wave, and heavy metal music. So, just as in any other generation, teenagers found new ways to annoy their parents and rebel in their own style.

Revolution in Music and Video Technology

The 1960s was a time of long-playing vinyl albums and big, clunky record players. The seventies gave people eight-track tapes, and later, cassette tapes and portable players. The 1980s saw a revolution in technology that changed how people listened to music and what they watched on television.

In 1982 the Japanese firm Sony launched the first line of compact disc (CD) players. CDs use laser technology to reproduce recorded music of a much higher quality than can be obtained from tapes and vinyl records.

Another revolution was represented by the personal stereo. Once again, Sony took the lead, introducing the Walkman in 1978. During the eighties, cheap copies of the Walkman were produced for the first time and ordinary teenagers could tune out the world with their own set of headphones. With stereo headsets, people could pursue their individual interests without disturbing whoever might be sitting next to them. This led to an increase in cassette sales, which outsold record albums for the first time. And personal stereos were perfect for a growing fad of the eighties—jogging.

Cable TV also appeared for the first time in the 1980s. Since 1950, most Americans only had three to five television channels to choose from. Cable displayed dozens of channels specializing in everything from movies to news to sports. And it could all be accessed by the flick of the newly introduced re-

A woman listens to music on her personal stereo while skating around a lake near her home in 1981. Personal stereos revolutionized the music industry by allowing people to take their music anywhere easily.

mote control clicker. By 1985, over half of all American homes had cable TV. When the videocassette recorder (VCR) entered widespread production, another viewing option was added to America's formerly limited TV menu.

MTV

The most important of outlets for eighties music was MTV, or Music Television, a cable television network that began broadcasting on August 1, 1981.

Before MTV there was *Popclips,* a music-video show dreamed up by Michael Nesmith, who was famous in the sixties as a member of the pop group the Monkees. *Popclips,* featured standup comic Howie Mandel as its sole videodisc jockey, or VJ. It was shown on Warner Cable's Nickelodeon cable television channel.

Warner realized the possibilities of a considerably more toned down, demographics-minded version of this mating of rock music and television, and allotted $20 million in startup costs to give birth to what became MTV. Since their artists financed videos as promotional items, it was MTV's initial masterstroke to convince the major labels that allowing the cable channel to broadcast these minimovies at no fee to MTV amounted to invaluable free advertising for the labels and musicians.[52]

MTV was targeted at twelve- to thirty-four-year-olds, who would think of the channel as a television version of a radio station.

Although it brought music videos into America's living rooms, not everyone was thrilled with MTV. One critic wrote:

> With the public's attention span shrinking by the second, cable's first 24-hour music channel establishes the four-minute rock video—essentially a commercial for an album—as the hot new art form. Fast cuts, slow motion, and artsy black-and-white photography—all selling sex and violence—define the visual style of the decade, spreading to movies, prime time series, advertising, and magazines.[53]

Rockin' into the Eighties

In the 1960s, rock music represented rebellion in its purest form. Musicians sang about ending the war, loving their fellow humans, and expanding their consciousness. By the mid-1970s rock's themes were considerably softened to achieve mass acceptance. What was considered "selling out" in the sixties simply became the thing to do in the seventies.

"The notion of rock as mainstream entertainment was gaining ground steadily. Rock became a reference point for a splintered culture."[54] But as in other parts of the business world, record companies were undergoing major consolidation. In 1980 the rock market was controlled by six major companies. With so few labels available,

Assassination of John Lennon

Nothing better signified the end of the peace-and-love sixties than the assassination of former Beatle John Lennon. Ken Tucker writes about the event in *Rock of Ages*.

Soon after rock music hauled itself into the 1980s it received the most jolting shock of all: the murder of John Lennon. In September 1980, Lennon and [his wife] Yoko Ono signed with Geffen Records and two months later released *Double Fantasy*, a Number One album with a Number One single, "(Just Like) Starting Over." Then on December 8, 1980, Lennon was shot seven times outside the Dakota, the apartment building he lived in [in New York City], by Mark David Chapman, a twenty-five-year-old Beatle fan.

Lennon's death was a crucial event in rock culture. Unlike Elvis Presley (the only other comparable example in cultural outreach and musical importance), Lennon might easily have pursued a long creative career. Moreover, the fact that Lennon was murdered by a self-professed fan made horrifyingly true all the paranoid fantasies that both pop stars and their audiences might have about the love/hate nature of rock-and-roll prominence.

After hearing the news of John Lennon's death, sympathetic crowds line the streets outside the Dakota, the luxury apartment building where Lennon lived and where he was murdered. Memorial services for the slain rock star were held throughout the world in the days following his assassination.

Lennon's death was the ultimate example of the era's fragmentation. All the media pundits repeated the same phrase—"The dream is over"—and it was: Rock fans were now forever separated from the myth of the Beatles. There was nothing left but to face the future.

there weren't many recording artists willing to take chances.

The money was piling up fast for huge established rock acts like Fleetwood Mac, REO Speedwagon, and Journey. Then along came punk rock. This raucous style of music featured stripped-down arrangements, loud abrasive vocals, and lyrics meant to shock.

> Punk attempted to restore to rock everything its success as a mass phenomenon was draining from it, most of all, the now nearly quaint notion that anyone could make music. Punk was a reaction to the increasing pride in technical virtuosity that was overrunning rock on every level, from the elaborate instruments used to create the music to the scientifically researched ways a major rock tour was mounted and executed. Punk was rock's most notable attempt to inject angry, rebellious, risk-taking notions into the music.[55]

By the 1980s punk bands like the Sex Pistols and the Clash had self-destructed. But the ideas put forth by the punks were taken into the eighties by people of broader talent and vision. Elvis Costello, David Byrne and the Talking Heads, The Cars, and the Pretenders took a no-nonsense ap-

proach to music and climbed into the Top Ten. The growth of small, independent college radio stations gave many of these new-wave bands airplay that they would not have had otherwise.

Michael Jackson

Some rock historians credit one person with the salvation of the 1980s rock in-

Michael Jackson was the most important pop rock star of the 1980s. Not only was his music innovative and popular, his videos, the first to tell full-length stories using his songs, were unusual and intriguing.

dustry. This artist sold an unprecedented number of records and revitalized an industry with the release of a single album. He turned the eyes of the media on himself and made rock the center of youth culture once again. His name was Michael Jackson.

Jackson recorded *Off the Wall* with Quincy Jones as producer in 1979. It sold 6 million copies, making it the biggest selling album ever recorded by an African-American artist. Fame and fortune, however, did not make Jackson very happy. At the time he said, "I believe I am one of the loneliest people in the world."[56]

Jackson's next album, *Thriller,* entered the *Billboard* Top Ten on January 3, 1983, where it stayed for seventy-eight weeks—occupying number one for thirty-seven weeks. Before the decade was over, *Thriller* had sold over 40 million copies and become the best-selling record album of all time. At one point it was selling a million copies a week. In March 1984 Jackson won a record eight Grammys for the album. Jackson released videos of three singles, "Billie Jean," "Beat It," and "Thriller." They set the standard for high-quality, well-produced videos on MTV.

In 1985, after watching news footage of starving people in Ethiopia, Jackson wrote "We Are the World" with Lionel Richie. Forty-five rock and pop stars gathered to record the song, including Bob Dylan, Ray Charles, Billy Joel, Cyndi Lauper, Bette Midler, Willie Nelson, Paul Simon, Bruce Springsteen, Stevie Wonder, and Tina Turner. On April 5, 1985, at 3:50 P.M. Greenwich Mean Time, five thousand radio stations across the globe played "We Are the World." A year after its release, the song had raised over $44 million for starving people in Africa.

Live Aid

Jackson's efforts inspired a worldwide outpouring of relief for Africa. In July 1985, Live Aid—one of the biggest events in rock history—was simultaneously held in London and Philadelphia. The concert was attended by 160,000 fans while another 1.5 billion watched it on TV or listened on the radio in 130 countries.

The concert was organized by Irish musician Bob Geldof and featured David Bowie, Elvis Costello, Tina Turner (singing with Mick Jagger), Phil Collins (who hopped the supersonic Concord to play in both cities), Paul McCartney (in his first live appearance in seven years), Bob Dylan (backed by Keith Richards and Ron Wood of the Rolling Stones), and Robert Plant and Jimmy Page (in their first reunion since the breakup of Led Zeppelin). Hundreds of thousands of people raised

Prince

In the mid-1980s, African-American artists dominated the Top Ten as they had not done since the 1960s. Lionel Richie, Tina Turner, Rick James, Billie Ocean, and the enduring Stevie Wonder all had number one hits in 1984. One of the most flamboyant artists of the time was Prince Rogers Nelson. Fred Bronson details Prince's rise to fame in *The Billboard Book of Number One Hits.*

Few performers in recent rock annals have engendered the peculiar mix of controversy, mystique and popularity created by Prince Rogers Nelson. (Prince is now referred to as "the Artist.") Termed at various times a prodigy, sinner, saint, genius or dictator, Prince was born June 7, 1960, in Minneapolis, Minnesota. The teenaged Prince led a migratory home existence. Eventually he wound up in the basement of Andre Cymone, Prince's best friend and later band mate. Outfitting the cellar in rabbit fur and mirrors, the visitor holed up at age 16, writing as many as three or four songs a day. They were "All fantasies. Because I didn't have anything around me . . . there are no people. No anything. When I started writing, I cut myself off from relationships." He also taught himself guitar, keyboards, drums and just about any other instrument he could get his hands on (over 27 in all) The one-man band rapidly conceived his own demonstration tapes.

Prince's shocking lyrics and unconventional style propelled him into the pop charts in the 1980s.

Eventually they solicited him a recording contract with Warner Brothers.

Prince's autobiographical movie *Purple Rain*, released in 1984, was called the best rock film ever made.

their voices together to end the show with "We Are the World." By early 1986, Live Aid had raised over $80 million which went to seven African nations: Ethiopia, Mozambique, Chad, Burkina Faso, Niger, Mali, and Sudan.

Women in Rock

The 1980s was a great decade for women in rock. The first women superstars were inspired by the punk scene in New York. Poet and protopunk Patti Smith began performing at the New York club CBGB (country, blue grass, and blues) in the 1970s. Blondie, fronted by Debbie Harry, started per-

forming there in 1977. By 1979 Harry was the punk pinup queen who was paving the way for other women in rock's male-dominated world. When Blondie released *Heart of Glass,* the band crossed over from punk to pop. Most of white America heard rap music for the first time when Blondie released their hit "Rapture" in 1981.

MTV opened up many opportunities for women to assert their personalities and their sexuality, as men had been doing for decades. One person who took full advantage of that opening was Tina Turner. Turner had spent the 1950s and the 1960s singing

Tina Turner sings at the 1985 Grammy Awards, where she won a Grammy for best pop female vocalist. Turner transformed her career as part of a duo with Ike Turner to become an even more popular solo performer.

rhythm-and-blues songs and dancing up a storm for the Ike and Tina Turner Revue. After leaving an abusive marriage to Ike in 1975, Turner released *Private Dancer* in 1984 and became world famous in a matter of months. The "bright smile and leggy look she emphasized onstage found its way onto scores of magazine covers."[57] *Private Dancer* sold in the millions.

Cyndi Lauper was another MTV success story of the 1980s. Her debut album, *She's So Unusual,* sold 3 million copies in 1984.

With her clear, strong voice and strikingly odd image—thrift-shop-elegant clothes, multi-color hair, exaggerated New Yawk speaking voice—Lauper seemed an exotic yet unpretentious figure. For all her wackiness, Lauper offered a significant alternative to the other female rock stars of the day. She completely by-passed the woman-as-sex-object stereotype

Cyndi Lauper holds the American Music Awards that she won in 1985 for best female vocalist and best female video artist.

that virtually all female rockers must confront.[58]

Madonna Ciccone, on the other hand, took the woman-as-sex-object ploy to new heights. "She had been a favorite in disco circles for a full two years before her cooing voice and commanding sartorial style (layered gypsy dresses, tons of bangles, exposed navel) attracted the attention of the mainstream pop audience." In 1984 her album *Like a Virgin* created Madonnamania. She found herself singing to prepubescent audiences who dressed just like she did—a *Time* magazine story on the singer dubbed the fans "Madonna Wanna-bes." [59] In 1985 Madonna starred in her first movie, *Desperately Seeking Susan.*

Madonna on stage at LIVE AID, a benefit to feed starving people in Africa in 1985. Madonna, a popular 1980s icon, continues to transform and change her music.

Blockbuster Movies

When VCRs were first sold, Hollywood producers worried that people would stop going out to theaters to see movies. But the new video player had the opposite effect. It fueled a boom in the motion picture business, which prospered and grew in the 1980s. Of the fifty most successful films ever made, half were produced during that decade.

The most popular movie of the 1980s was Steven Spielberg's *E.T., the*

Extra-Terrestrial. "Recent figures show that $229 million was spent on tickets to see the small alien with the appetite for candy, who merely wanted to 'phone home.'"[60]

Other top-grossing movies of the 1980s included George Lucas's *The Empire Strikes Back* (1980) and *Return of the Jedi* (1983), *Batman* (1989), *Ghostbusters* (1984), and two more Spielberg offerings, *Raiders of the Lost Ark* (1981) and *Indiana Jones and the Last Crusade* (1989).

While fantasy and science fiction filled the screens, tough guys like Clint Eastwood, Sylvester Stallone, Chuck Norris, and Arnold Schwarzenegger pumped out plenty of violence, action, and gore. From the darkly nasty science fiction thriller *Terminator* in 1984, Schwarzenegger, with his thick Austrian accent, continued with "splatter" movies such as *Commando, Predator,* and *The Running Man.* Critics panned these movies for their hyperviolence, but they sold millions of tickets worldwide.

Sylvester Stallone became something of a folk hero playing a vengeful Vietnam War veteran in *First Blood, Rambo,* and *Rambo II. Rambo* opened in a record number of theaters and grossed $32.5 million in its first six days.

While Hollywood churned out the blockbusters, young African-American director Spike Lee drew popular and critical acclaim with low-budget hits such as *She's Gotta Have It* and *Do the Right Thing,* which examined sex, race

Arnold Schwarzenegger strikes a familiar pose—holding a weapon while waiting to ambush an evil villain. Schwarzenegger became popular in violent thrillers such as Terminator, Predator, *and* Commando.

relations, interracial love, and other themes rarely found on the big screen in the 1980s.

Eighties Television

Television aired a growing number of shows with black stars in the 1980s. No one was more successful than Bill Cosby, whose *Bill Cosby Show* was the top-rated show of the decade.

The eighties saw many firsts on TV. The Iran hostage crisis gave rise to Ted Koppel's *Nightline*. The news talk show opened every night by reciting how many days the crisis had been going on. ("This is day 247 in the Iran hostage crisis.") Some linked Koppel's relentless coverage of the hostages' ordeal to Jimmy Carter's defeat in the 1980 presidential election.

On a less serious note, *Miami Vice*, which debuted in 1984, made a star of Don Johnson in a show about Miami detectives dressed in designer fashions. *The Golden Girls* premiered in 1985 and was the first show whose stars were well into their fifties and sixties. *Thirtysomething* appeared on the air in 1987 and ad-

Censoring Rock Music

As in earlier decades, 1980s rock came under fire from politicians who were upset about sex and violence in music and videos. In the book *The Clothes Have No Emperor*, Paul Slansky lists a few quotes overheard at the Senate Commerce Committee hearings on dirty rock lyrics. The comments are from Tipper Gore (Vice President Albert Gore's wife) and Frank Zappa, rock composer and founder of The Mothers of Invention. They were testifying before Missouri Republican John Danforth and Al Gore, who was the democratic senator from Tennessee at the time.

"Children in the vulnerable age brackets have a natural love for music. If, as a parent, you believe they should be exposed to something more uplifting than 'Sugar Walls,' support music appreciation programs in schools."—Frank Zappa

"Let me say, although I disagree with some of the statements you make, I have been a fan of your music, believe it or not, and I respect you as a true original and tremendously talented musician."—Senator Al Gore to Frank Zappa

"Excuse me, are you gonna tell me you're a big fan of my music as well?"—Dee Snider of Twisted Sister to Al Gore, who admitted he is "not a fan."

"There is nothing on the album cover which would notify you if the record has pornographic material or material glorifying violence."—Senator John Danforth.

"No, there is nothing that would suggest that to me."—Tipper Gore.

"I would say that a buzz saw blade between the guy's legs on the album cover is a good indication that it's not for little Johnny."—Frank Zappa.

dressed the concerns of the baby boom generation coming to terms with growing older.

In 1987, a fourth network, Fox, went on the air to compete with CBS, NBC, and ABC. Fox began with only seven stations but soon became available via cable and independent stations. Before the end of the decade, 90 percent of American homes were able to tune into Fox, whose cartoon series *The Simpsons* seriously challenged *Cosby* on Thursday nights. And the upstart network changed the way network television looked with hits like *In Living Color.*

Talk shows flooded onto the airwaves in the eighties. David Letterman got his start when *Late Night* began in 1982. By 1989 Oprah Winfrey, Geraldo Rivera, Sally Jessy Raphael, Pat Sajak, Arsenio Hall, and Larry King and others all hosted popular talk shows.

Members of the cast of the popular Bill Cosby Show *pose for a publicity shot.*

The Growth of AM Radio

The talk show phenomenon went beyond television in the eighties and crossed over to AM radio. With FM radio stations given over to rock and country music, AM radio began to attract conservative, older, and more religious listeners. Many stations hired right-wing conservatives like Rush Limbaugh, Pat Buchanan, and G. Gordon Liddy, who had served a prison sentence for his role in the Watergate break-in of 1972. Limbaugh and others attracted sizable audiences by their harsh, often exaggerated criticisms of women, liberals, Democrats, and environmentalists.

Until the 1980s, American television and radio broadcasters were obligated by law to avoid blatant partisan politics, neither supporting nor impugning any politician. The rule was called the "fairness doctrine."

The Reagan FCC (Federal Communications Commission) was the first to vote to abolish the agency's longstanding fairness doctrine, which required broadcasters to air controversial issues by providing a balanced presentation of public issues. There was no doubt about the overall effect. Driven by bottomline profits, the networks and their new corporate managers eagerly responded to the new climate of deregulation. They gave the public what they thought it wanted—and whatever led to greater audience ratings and higher profits. Increasingly even the news divisions were dragged into the ratings battle and pressured to produce greater profits.[61]

American Pop Culture Goes Global

American popular culture invaded the four corners of the globe in the eighties. From Michael Jackson to *Rambo,* and from MTV to the Simpsons, the products, fashions, and fads churned out by America's entertainment industry traveled to India, Hong Kong, Europe, and even the Soviet Union. This globalization of Hollywood values appalled some critics but made billions of dollars for entertainers from the United States.

Chapter Six

Steve Jobs (left) and Steve Wozniak (right) were instrumental in launching the era of the desktop computer. Here they are shown with then Apple president John Sculley at a product launch for the Apple II.

Technology and Science

The 1980s saw advances in science and technology that created a watershed between the old and the new. Cars became more fuel efficient, were built better, and lasted longer. In medicine, research into diet and health showed people how to live longer by eating better. And the personal computer revolution changed the way people worked and communicated.

Autos in the Eighties

The American auto industry has always been one of the nation's best economic indicators. When the auto business does well, it means the economy is healthy. And Americans love their cars.

The automobile was the product that expressed what America thought of itself and enabled it to change so rapidly. Nothing typified the American ideal of individual freedom and mobility, size and speed better than ownership of the most luxurious car—the bigger and more powerful, the better. And by the eighties nothing symbolized the industrial decline of the United States more than its automobile industry.[62]

In the 1980s Japanese auto sales passed American auto sales for the first time. Detroit auto executives, however, dismissed the notion that European and Japanese cars could ever replace their product. "I can assure you that most executives and dealers in luxury cars back in the seventies had never sat inside a small or European car—or even considered that they were transportation,"[63] said Cadillac's chief engineer, Robert Templin.

Even skyrocketing fuel prices in the mid-1970s failed to change the auto industry's concepts of design and engineering. But the spiral of inflation that had helped to propel Reagan into the White House also battered the auto industry: supplies were up, sales were down, and layoffs increased. Rising energy prices also drove up the costs of materials needed to build autos. Said Cadillac's Templin [at the time]:

The readily available materials are far more expensive, and of course,

the capacity of the world to produce materials has not grown nearly as fast. Ten years ago, for instance, we didn't have to worry about how much steel we used. Now you no longer can say you're going to use all the steel there is, or all the glass, or all the aluminum.[64]

A second fuel crisis in 1979 brought an abrupt increase in consumer demand for compact and even subcompact cars. America's auto industry did not respond to the growing demand, producing instead smaller cars of lower quality than the Japanese compacts. By 1980 Japan had captured 25 percent of the total U.S. car market while Swedish and German cars were taking a significant portion of the luxury market.

The U.S. auto industry went on a major modernizing binge, spending $69 billion worldwide to redesign products and modernize plants, many of which had been built before World War II. In 1984 the American auto industry began to rebound, and its cars were once again selling well. The introduction of the minivan and the smaller pickup truck spurred sales. As the decade progressed, American carmakers began to satisfy concerns for safety and comfort by improving windshields, safety belts, head restraints, brakes, tires, lighting, door strength, and roof strength.

Toyota trucks are unloaded in Baltimore. Japanese automakers' fuel-efficient and dependable vehicles allowed them to top the sales of American manufacturers during the 1980s.

Environmental Disasters

The 1980s were marked with several huge environmental disasters—both natural and man-made. On May 18, 1980, Mount St. Helens—a long-dormant volcano in the state of Washington—erupted with a force five hundred times greater than that of the atomic bomb dropped on Hiroshima during World War II. It was the most violent volcanic event to take place in the continental United States. The explosion reduced the mountain's height by thirteen hundred feet and destroyed $3 billion worth of forest and agricultural land. Although the public was notified that the mountain was going to explode, many people refused to leave the area, and sixty deaths were reported. As the side of the mountain blew up, smoke and ash billowed miles into the air, affecting the world's weather for several years.

The other great natural disaster occurred at the opposite end of the decade and hundreds of miles down the coast. On October 17, 1989, millions of Americans were watching TV awaiting the start of the World Series baseball game in San Francisco. Suddenly a powerful earthquake measuring 6.9 on the Richter scale rocked the area. The rumble only lasted a few seconds, but the force of the quake collapsed freeways and buildings. A total of sixty-six people died as commuters on their way home from work were caught on buckling freeways and collapsing bridges.

In addition to natural catastrophes, several environmental disasters were attributed to human beings. The worst commercial nuclear accident at the time took place at Three Mile Island in Pennsylvania in 1979. Workers at nuclear plants were contaminated in Tennessee in 1981, in New York in 1982, and in Oklahoma in 1986. Also in 1986, a world away, the Chernobyl nuclear plant exploded in the Soviet Union. Massive amounts of radioactivity were released as the power plant spewed radiation across several countries.

Meanwhile, residents in the ironically named Love Canal area were fighting another kind of pollution. Love Canal is a body of water near a residential section of Niagara Falls, New York. Residents of the modest ranch houses in the area learned that the Hooker Chemical Company had dumped twenty-one thousand tons of dioxins—a chemical waste—in the canal between 1942 and 1953. The state of New York purchased all 789 houses in the area, which were then demolished. Tons of sod, clay, and plastic were brought in to fill a ditch three thousand feet long by one hundred feet wide, by forty feet deep.

The *Exxon Valdez* Oil Spill

By the end of the 1980s, Americans were using more gasoline than ever. This consumption led oil companies to provide more oil at a faster rate, which sometimes led to increased accidents.

In March 1989, the oil tanker *Exxon Valdez* went off course and struck a reef in the pristine waters of Prince William Sound, Alaska. More than 240,000 barrels, or over 11 million gallons, of crude oil spilled over a 1,600-square-mile area, contaminating more than 800 miles of shoreline of one of the world's richest wildlife areas. Commercial fishing was devastated as the thick crude oil spread through the waters, and Alaskan wildlife was destroyed in horrific numbers.

The captain of the huge tanker had a known history of alcoholism that included several arrests for drunken driving. When a blood test was taken nine hours after the accident, the captain still had an unacceptable level of alcohol in his system. In difficult waters, the drunk captain turned the *Valdez* over to an uncertified third mate.

Exxon, the world's largest company, had not prepared a thorough, detailed contingency plan to deal with potentially large oil spills. As the immensity of the disaster became evident, consumers, environmentalists, and politicians vented their anger at the giant corporation, initiating boycotts of Exxon products. Exxon admitted that consumers had returned more than eighteen thousand credit cards.

But while the focus of America was on the oil spills and earthquakes, another industry was forming in small

The Exxon Valdez *oil spill covered the rocks and animals of Prince William Sound, Alaska, for miles. (Above) Exxon cleanup workers use high-pressure water to push oil from rocks back into the ocean where it can be collected. (Left) Joseph Hazelwood was captain of the* Exxon Valdez *when it ran aground in 1989.*

warehouses and offices in California. And its creativity and innovation would change the very shape of the modern world.

Computers Everywhere

The beginning of the personal computer age was marked in 1975 when a small firm introduced the Altair 8800, which had enough memory to store about one paragraph of written material. The Altair used an Intel microprocessor and was offered as a $399 do-it-yourself kit. But the Altair was soon forgotten, and by 1980 the computer world was domi-

nated by two college dropouts named Steve Jobs and Steve Wozniak. Wozniak and Jobs started the revolutionary Apple Computer Company in 1976 after building a prototype user-friendly computer. Wozniak concentrated on research and technology while Jobs concentrated on marketing. By 1984 Apple had become a billion-dollar company and was largely responsible for the microcomputer explosion of the late 1970s and early 1980s.

The Apple II was the first personal computer (PC), and it sold in the millions (a modified version of Apple II was

A computer inventor shows off his new game for the Apple II computer system, the first personal computer. The invention of small, user-friendly personal computers transformed the home and the workplace.

sold until 1994). Apples were the first machines to be used in schools to instruct children in computer use. In 1983 Apple brought out the Lisa model computer. Lisa, the first computer with a mouse, had a memory that is tiny by today's standards: one megabyte of RAM and two megabytes of ROM. It cost $10,000.

Industrial giant IBM had been in the computer industry since 1953. But it didn't enter the personal computer race until 1981. Other electronics firms that were early competitors were Commodore, Atari, Tandy, Timex, and Texas Instruments.

The rapid emergence of the computer industry was not going unnoticed. In January 1983, *Time* magazine broke with fifty-five years of tradition by featuring the personal computer as "Machine of the Year," in place of its usual "Man of the Year." As author Otto Friedrich said:

> There are some occasions . . . when the most significant force in a year's news is not a single individual but a process, and a widespread recognition by a whole society that this process is changing the course of all other processes. This is why, after weighing the ebb and flow of events around the world . . . *Time's* Man of the Year for 1982 . . . is not a man at all. It is a machine: the computer.[65]

As more and more people bought computers the prices fell dramatically. Apple's model IIe sold for as little as $1,000. More sophisticated computers, however, carried price tags of up to $30,000—or about $55,000 in today's dollars. Some 2.8 million computers sold in 1982, in a market worth $4.9 billion. By 1990, almost 40 percent of PCs were linked by telephone lines to other PCs in local networks.

By 1990, the worldwide personal computer market was fueling a $70 billion-a-year industry. A growing demand for computer hardware such as central processors, modems, monitors, and printers gave rise to dozens of secondary businesses that created jobs and helped the economy to grow.

The importance of the personal computer cannot be overstated. At first the machines were complicated and expensive and confined to use by businesses. But the user-friendly features pioneered by the Palo Alto Research Center of Xerox (Xerox PARC), Apple, and others removed the mystery from computers and made them household items.

Computer Software

As time passed, software (the programs used to run computers) became as important as hardware (the computers themselves). The first popular software programs were geared toward business.

Computers from Grains of Sand

The brain of every computer is its silicon chip. Silicon is simply a chemical element that can be purified and formatted into tiny wafers called chips, which are then covered with semiconductors. The first silicon chip, assembled by electronics wizard Jack Kilby at Texas Instruments in 1958, allowed several electronic components to be placed in a single piece of semiconductor. In 1971 Intel Corporation produced an integrated circuit that could make all the decisions in a computer. This little unit became known as the microprocessor or microchip.

David Wright explains the process in his book *Computers.*

> The concentration of so many transistors in a single chip has several advantages, including the ability to process information at a high speed. A microchip the size of a penny may contain more than two hundred thousand transistors. Not only did its creation reduce the size, weight, and power consumption of computers, it reduced the cost.

By the end of the eighties, handheld games, automotive emissions systems, and ballistic missiles were among the devices being run by these tiny forms of artificial intelligence.

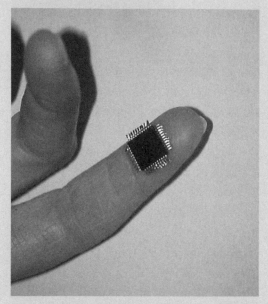

A person holds a computer microchip on the tip of his finger. The tiny chip was responsible for revolutionizing the way data is stored.

Visicalc, introduced in 1979, was an early spreadsheet program. Aldus Page-Maker, which allows artists, printers, and graphic designers to lay out book, magazine, and newspaper pages, paved the way for desktop publishing, a multibillion-dollar industry.

At that time, Microsoft was a small computer firm founded by William "Bill" Henry Gates III and Paul Allen. But in 1980, Microsoft obtained an operating system that had been developed by IBM for $50,000. It was called "86-DOS." Microsoft made adjustments and changed the software's name to MS-DOS. In one of the costliest mistakes in the history of capitalism, IBM failed to retain the exclusive rights to license the DOS system, and by 1993, Microsoft was the computer industry's richest company, almost 90 percent of the world's computers ran on MS-DOS, and Bill Gates was one of the world's richest people.

The late eighties saw a widespread computerization of jobs and services of many kinds. For the first time, people were able to check airline schedules, rent cars, order flowers, send gifts, and seek information from their desk at home or at work.

Development of the Internet

The Internet as it exists today is a massive but relatively easy-to-use network of computers hooked together by phone lines. At the beginning of the eighties, however, Internet access was available only to government employees, the military, and university research departments.

The Defense Department started the Internet in the early 1970s as the Advanced Research Projects Agency network, ARPAnet. This network was implemented to support military communications in the event of partial power outages due to war or sabotage. By the early 1980s, there were many local area networks [LANs], primarily for PC users. Internet access via the LANs was then possible.

In the late 1980s, five extremely expensive regional supercomputer centers were created by the National Science Foundation (NSF) to make the world's fastest computers available for academic research. The NSF built its own network with connections running at roughly 56,000 bits per second (56 kbps) over specially conditioned telephone lines. This is slow by today's

Bill Gates, one of the wealthiest men in the world, established his company by buying already developed software, improving it, and parlaying it into the standard of the industry.

standards—only about two pages per second could be transmitted—but there were high costs for special phone lines, since telephone companies charge for these lines by the mile. To cut expenses, the NSF created regional networks that connected to their nearest neighbor, in daisy-chain fashion. This allowed any computer to communicate with any other computer in the network by passing messages up and down the chain. This strategy was so successful that the network quickly became overloaded by researchers sharing resources not directly related to the objectives of the supercomputer centers.

By the end of the decade, the original NSF network was replaced with telephone lines that were twenty times faster. Quicker computers were also added. The network then was opened to most academic researchers, international research organizations, and government employees and contractors. By the early 1990s, the network was opened to a few commercial sites and international Internet access expanded rapidly. Today, the Internet is a collection of high-speed networks composed of the national backbone network provided by the National Science Foundation.

The Space Program

Average Americans were discovering computers in the 1980s, but the amaz-ing machines had been used in the space program since the 1960s. As computer technology grew, the National Aeronautics and Space Administration (NASA) was able to conquer bigger and more difficult challenges. NASA's crowning achievement in the 1980s was the space shuttle.

Space shuttles were the first reusable spacecraft. They acted as launch vehicles, platforms for scientific laboratories, orbiting service centers for satellites, and return carriers for spacecraft that had been in orbit. In short, the space shuttle was a space truck that could carry cargo to and from outer space.

The first space shuttle to leave the ground was *Columbia*, which rose from the launch pad at Cape Canaveral on April 12, 1981. *Columbia* made a safe landing two days later, touching down at Edwards Air Force Base in California. *Columbia* flew three more test flights before deploying two commercial communications satellites on November 11–16, 1982.

Unfortunately for NASA and supporters of the space program, the early 1980s saw flagging public support and shrinking budgets. After the last moon landing in 1975, senators and citizens began to question why billions of dollars were used to send people into space. Television audiences for space

The space shuttle Columbia *returns to Edwards Air Force Base after its historic space flight.*

launches fell to record lows. To revive interest for the shuttle program, NASA decided to publicize a series of launches that would capture the country's attention.

America's interest in the space program increased dramatically when the first flight of the space shuttle *Challenger* carried physicist Dr. Sally Ride into space on April 4–9, 1983. Ride was the first American woman to fly in space (two Soviet women had already gained cosmonaut status). NASA made history once again on August 30, 1983, when Guion S. Bluford Jr., aboard *Challenger*, became the first African American to travel into space. Ride became the first woman to travel into space two times when she flew on the *Challenger* on October 5-13, 1984.

Challenger Disaster

January 28, 1986, was to be the silver anniversary for the space shuttle program—flight number 25. It was a clear, bright morning at Cape Canaveral as seven members of the shuttle crew were strapped into their seats. Among the crew were Judith A. Resnik, the second American woman in space, and Christa McAuliffe, a New Hampshire schoolteacher. McAuliffe was NASA's first space shuttle pas-

senger in the Teachers in Space program. The thirty-seven-year-old teacher planned to teach her class from the shuttle, during a live TV transmission. NASA's inclusion of McAuliffe—the first civilian in space—sparked the interest of the entire country.

Thousands of people at Cape Canaveral were joined by millions of television viewers tuned in to watch the $1.2 billion *Challenger* take off at 11:38 A.M. The launch went smoothly, but when the shuttle reached an altitude of 47,000 feet and was traveling

The seven-member crew of the space shuttle Challenger *included teacher Christa McAuliffe (first woman on left). Their tragic flight, in which all of them died when the* Challenger *exploded, left Americans in shock and wondering who was at fault.*

The space shuttle Challenger *moments before it would explode in midair, instantly killing all seven crew members.*

aboard died. The two solid rocket boosters were sent zigzagging wildly through the sky as America watched on in horror.

The *Challenger* explosion shook the country. Five days later, fifteen thousand people turned out for a memorial service for the astronauts in Houston. In New Hampshire, more than a thousand people attended a memorial service for McAuliffe. In Los Angeles, 1.2 million schoolchildren observed a moment of silence in honor of McAuliffe.

The tragedy marked the greatest loss of life suffered in the history of American space exploration. On June 13, 1986, President Reagan ordered NASA to redesign the boosters on the shuttle. Over the next several years, four hundred changes were made to the vehicle.

NASA went ahead with its space shuttle mission. In 1988, *Discovery* completed a successful mission. In 1989 *Atlantis* placed the first planetary observatory in space—the *Magellan* radar imaging spacecraft. *Magellan* later sent back beautiful pictures of Venus.

Advances in Medicine

faster than the speed of sound, at 1,977 miles per hour, a small flame seemed to erupt from the rocket booster. Fifteen seconds later, a huge explosion ignited half a million gallons of fuel. *The Challenger* was blown to bits. All those

As the space shuttle program grew and died and grew again, great strides were being made in various fields of medicine. Although cancer rates rose slightly throughout the decade, by

1989 scientists had discovered that certain people were predisposed to cancer because of their genetic inheritance. They also learned that there might never be a single cure for cancer because the disease has so many different forms.

There were some positive signs, however. There was a decline in respiratory cancers among young people because tobacco use had gone down. There was a rise in reported breast cancer among older women, but researchers believed that careful self-examination and scheduled checkups were partly responsible for the upward trend. As health- and weight-conscious Americans began eating lower fat diets, digestive tract cancers declined.

Death rates from heart disease—another major killer—declined about 20 and 10 percent, respectively, for males and females during the 1980s. Besides benefiting from increased knowledge about diet and exercise, more heart-attack victims were surviving because of better emergency procedures:

Physicians armed with everything from laser beams to space-age imaging machines could watch a patient's heartbeat on a screen as they injected dye and threaded tiny balloons into arteries to open clogged passageways. Heart-bypass surgery, unknown before the mid-

1960s, had a mortality rate of approximately 1.5 percent by the mid-1980s.[66]

Preventive medicine came to the forefront in 1984 when a ten-year study showed that heavy consumption of meat and dairy products increased cholesterol levels in the blood, putting people at greater risk for heart attacks. Doctors reported that a low-cholesterol diet of fruit, vegetables, bread, and pasta could reduce heart disease by 50 percent.

The Spread of AIDS

AIDS, the acquired immunodeficiency syndrome, was considered an epidemic for the first time in the 1980s. Figures released in 1990 show that the disease had killed 150,000 U.S. residents. Even more Americans carried the deadly human immunodeficiency virus (HIV) that causes the disease.

AIDS first surfaced in central Africa in the mid-1970s. People were coming down with rare forms of cancer, pneumonia, rashes, blindness, sores, and other disabling symptoms. AIDS spread to the United States, most notably in New York City and San Francisco. Many of the AIDS patients were homosexual men. Exchange of bodily fluids through sex was discovered to spread the disease. People in Haiti began to show symptoms as well, and doctors discovered that Haitians, who had picked up the infection while working in Africa, had brought the disease home. Others who caught AIDS were needle-sharing drug addicts and hospital patients who had received tainted blood transfusions. Author David Wright describes the varied responses to the epidemic in the United States:

> Like many things in the 1980s, AIDS took on a political spin. Gay activists blamed the conservative Reagan administration for not immediately pouring millions of research dollars into a fund to combat the disease. Administration officials, some of whom agreed that AIDS was a desperate emergency, were forced to remain silent because religious conservatives (who were Reagan supporters) saw the disease as a punishment from God for homosexuality. Conservative Christian influence forced the Department of Health and Human Services to drag its feet for several years as the disease spread, despite the efforts of C. Everett Koop, the surgeon general.[67]

And AIDS did spread rapidly. Blood banks could not screen the virus out of all of their blood, so people in hospitals

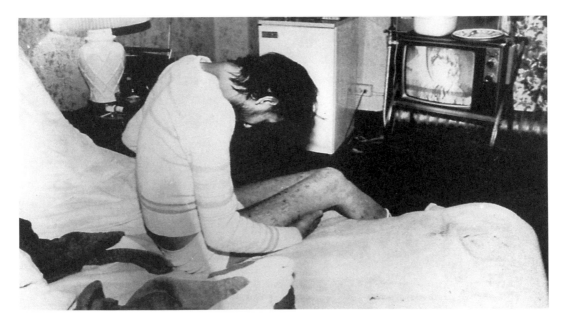

Destitute and covered with lesions, an AIDS victim sits alone in his hotel room. The disease spread rapidly during the 1980s, causing changes in sexual behavior among both homosexuals and heterosexuals.

for unrelated problems risked becoming infected with AIDS as a result of a transfusion of tainted blood. Another problem was the nature of the disease: an infected person can carry the virus for years before any symptoms appear.

AIDS had a tremendous influence on sexual behavior in the 1980s. Condoms became a requirement for casual sex. And by the end of the decade condoms were sold more openly in supermarkets and drugstores.

Ryan White

Initially many American heterosexual men and women took comfort from the belief that only homosexuals and people who injected themselves with illegal drugs were at risk of contracting AIDS. But when thirteen-year-old Ryan White caught AIDS from a blood-clotting drug he took to counter hemophilia, he gave AIDS an innocent face and aroused the compassion of many who had been ignoring the disease. The following extended quote from White comes from his testimony before the Presidential Commission on AIDS given in 1988.

> I came face to face with death at thirteen years old. I was diagnosed with AIDS: a killer. Doctors told me I'm not contagious. Given six months to live and being the fighter that I am, I set high goals for myself. It was my decision to live a normal life, go to school, be with my friends, and enjoy day to day activities. It was not going to be easy.
>
> The school I was going to said they had no guidelines for a person with AIDS. . . . We began a series of court battles for nine months, while I was attending classes by telephone. Eventually, I won the right to attend school, but the prejudice was still there. Listening to medical facts was not enough. People wanted one hundred percent guarantees. There are no one hundred percent guarantees in life, but concessions were made by mom and me to help ease the fear. We decided to meet everyone halfway. . . . Because of the lack of education on AIDS, discrimination, fear, panic, and lies surrounded me. (1) I became the target of Ryan White jokes. (2) Lies about me biting people. (3) Spitting on vegetables and cookies. (4) Urinating on bathroom walls. (5) Some restaurants threw away my dishes. (6) My school locker was vandalized inside and folders were marked FAG and other obscenities.[68]

White was labeled a troublemaker and his mom an unfit mother. When he entered a church or restaurant, people got up and left. This treatment led to televi-

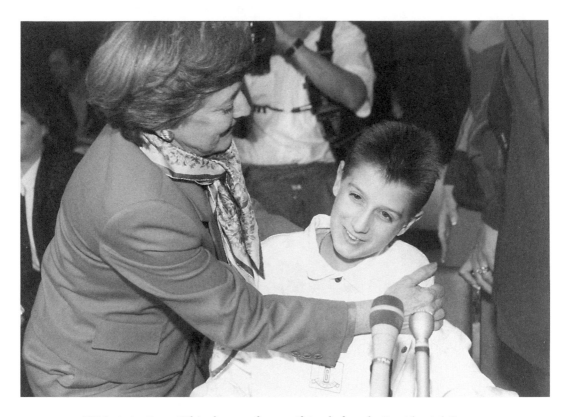

AIDS victim Ryan White leaves after testifying before the Presidential Commission on AIDS in Washington, D.C. White, who contracted the virus from a blood-clotting product used to treat his hemophilia, was shunned by people who did not fully understand how the disease could be transmitted.

sion interviews and dozens of public appearances. White became known as the AIDS boy. He received thousands of letters of support from around the world. Ryan White died from complications from AIDS at the age of eighteen.

Making Life Better

In the eighties, science offered two steps forward while nature forced one step backward. Automobiles were improved, but the bigger demand for oil caused increased air and water pollution. The remarkable space program offered people hope for the future, but its stability was called into question when the *Challenger* blew up over Florida. Medicine found new ways to save lives and offered research so people could heal themselves. But AIDS overshadowed medical advances and spawned a fear of sex.

Epilogue

Computer literacy has become a buzzword in the educational arena as schools across America scurry to upgrade their curriculums and place computers in the hands of teachers and students.

Into the Wired Decade

In 1990 the United States celebrated 214 years of the democratic experiment. It remained a society whose ideals of justice and freedom were emulated around the world. In all those years (except for the Civil War) the United States never experienced violent upheavals of the kind that have overthrown governments throughout history.

The 1980s showed that the system of checks and balances in the American system worked. Unethical behavior and criminal conduct in government resulted in prosecutions when the misdeeds were made public. On Wall Street, excessive greed was criticized, and insider traders were punished. Yet, ironically, while Americans took their freedoms for granted in the 1980s, people in Eastern Europe and China were laying down their lives to fight for American-style democracy.

A More Open Society

Many major news stories of the 1980s began in secret, far from public scrutiny. Events such as the Iran-Contra affair and the savings and loan scandal were not discovered until it was too late. But as the eighties turned into the nineties, it became harder and harder to keep a secret in America. The rise of cable news networks and the constant demand for stories by the voracious news media contributed to a more open society—for better or for worse. The growth of the Internet has allowed people to seek out information and carry on a nonstop conversation about world events, making the actions of politicians in slow-moving national legislatures increasingly irrelevant to people's daily lives.

The 1980s were the last years of the cold war. The superpower confrontation ended not with a bang but with a whimper. Most Americans never saw it coming. With the start of the

Two Harrisburg, Pennsylvania, middle school students show then governor Dick Thornburgh how to use one of their classroom computers.

new millennium, the fall of the Soviet Union will mark the end of the turbulent twentieth century better than any other signpost. As the threat from outside forces diminished, Americans seemed to be turning inward. They started pursuing their own interests via trillions of bytes zipping across phone lines. While leaving the bombs of the cold war behind, people hope to be riding the information superhighway into the future.

Notes

Introduction:
Summing Up the Seventies

1. Bruce Springsteen, "57 Channels (and Nothin' On)," *Human Touch*, 1992.
2. Bob Schieffer and Gary Paul Gates, *The Acting President.* New York: E. F. Dutton, 1989, p. 14.
3. Larry Beinhart, *American Hero.* New York: Pantheon Books, 1993, p. 123.
4. David Wright, *America in the 20th Century: 1980–1989.* New York: Marshall Cavendish, 1995, p. 1170.
5. Ronald Reagan, *An American Life.* New York: Simon & Schuster, 1990, p. 138.

Chapter One:
The Reagan Revolution

6. Quoted in *Congressional Quarterly* staff, *President Reagan.* Washington, DC: Government Printing Office, 1981, p. 9.
7. *Congressional Quarterly* staff, *President Reagan,* p. 9.
8. Quoted in *Congressional Quarterly* staff, *President Reagan,* p. 10.
9. Quoted in *Congressional Quarterly* staff, *President Reagan,* p.43.
10. Quoted in Schieffer and Gates, *The Acting President,* p. 141.
11. Quoted in Haynes Johnson, *Sleepwalking Through History.* New York: Anchor Books, 1992, p. 110.
12. Quoted in Bill Adler, ed., *The Uncommon Wisdom of Ronald Reagan.* Boston: Little, Brown, 1996, p. 50.
13. Quoted in *Congressional Quarterly staff, President Reagan,* p. 95.
14. Quoted in Ronnie Dugger, *On Reagan.* New York: McGraw-Hill, 1983, p. 287.
15. Quoted in Geraldine Baum, *Los Angeles Times,* April 3, 1998, p. 1.
16. Quoted in *Congressional Quarterly* staff, *President Reagan,* p. 22.
17. Quoted in *Congressional Quarterly* staff, *President Reagan,* p. 22.
18. Wright, *America in the 20th Century: 1980–1989,* p. 1265.
19. Schieffer and Gates, *The Acting President,* pp. 377–78.
20. Quoted in Roy Gutman, *Banana Diplomacy.* New York: Simon & Schuster, 1988, p. 338.
21. Quoted in AP writers, *The Reagan Era, 1981–1988,* p. 210.
22. Ann Wroe, *Lives, Lies, & the Iran-Contra Affair.* New York:

I. B. Tauris, 1991, pp. 55–56.

Chapter Two:
Final Curtain on Communism

23. Quoted in Peter Schweizer, *Victory.* New York: Atlantic Monthly Press, 1994, p. xi.
24. Quoted in Peter Schweizer, *Victory,* p. xii.
25. Quoted in AP writers, *The Reagan Era,* p. 50.
26. Quoted in Stuart Kallen, *Gorbachev/Yeltsin: The Fall of Communism.* Minneapolis: Abdo & Daughters, 1992, p. 18.
27. Quoted in Kallen, *Gorbachev/Yeltsin,* p. 26.
28. Kallen, *Gorbachev/Yeltsin,* p. 29.
29. AP writers, *An Uneasy Peace: 1988– .* New York: Grolier Press, 1995, p. 21.
30. Quoted in AP writers, *The Reagan Era,* p. 237.
31. Quoted in AP writers, *The Reagan Era,* p. 237.
32. Quoted in AP writers, *The Reagan Era,* p. 249.

Chapter Three:
Wall Street and Corporate Power

33. Quoted in Charles S. Bullock III, James E. Anderson, and David W. Brady, *Public Policy in the Eighties.* Monterey, CA: Brooks/Cole, 1983, p. 111.

34. Janet Lowe, *Secret Empire: How 25 Multinationals Rule the World.* Homewood, IL: Business One Irwin, 1992, p. 5.
35. Quoted in Marshall B. Clinard, *Corporate Corruption.* New York: Praeger, 1990, p. 28.
36. James B. Stewart, *Den of Thieves.* New York: Simon & Schuster, 1991, p. 83.
37. Quoted in Nathan Miller, *Stealing from America.* New York: Paragon House, 1992, p. 348.
38. Kathleen Day, *S&L Hell.* New York: W. W. Norton, 1993, p. 32.
39. Miller, *Stealing from America,* p. 350.
40. Quoted in Day, *S&L Hell,* p. 373.
41. Kevin Phillips, *The Politics of Rich and Poor.* New York: Random House, 1990, p. xvii.

Chapter Four:
Lives of Everyday People

42. Johnson, *Sleepwalking Through History,* p. 243.
43. Johnson, *Sleepwalking Through History,* p. 118.
44. Phillips, *The Politics of Rich and Poor,* pp. 14–15.
45. Quoted in Johnson, *Sleepwalking Through History,* p. 125.
46. Johnson, *Sleepwalking Through History,* p. 136.

■

47. Quoted in Wright, *America in the 20th Century: 1980–1989,* p. 1268.

48. Johnson, *Sleepwalking Through History,* p. 451.

49. Phillips, *The Politics of Rich and Poor,* p. 20.

50. Wright, *America in the 20th Century: 1980–1989,* pp. 1185–86.

Chapter Five:
Pop Culture: Off the Wall

51. Neil Howe and Bill Strauss, *13th Gen: Abort, Retry, Ignore, Fail?* New York: Vintage Books, 1993, p. 11.

52. Ed Ward, Geoffrey Stokes, and Ken Tucker, *Rock of Ages.* New York: Rolling Stone Press, 1986, p. 592.

53. Quoted in Paul Slansky, *The Clothes Have No Emperor.* New York: Fireside Books, 1989, p. 28.

54. Tucker, *Rock of Ages,* p. 520.

55. Tucker, *Rock of Ages,* p. 547.

56. Quoted in Stuart Kallen, *Retrospect of Rock.* Minneapolis: Abdo & Daughters, 1989, p. 27.

57. Tucker, *Rock of Ages,* p. 606.

58. Tucker, *Rock of Ages,* p. 606.

59. Tucker, *Rock of Ages,* p. 607.

60. Wright, *America in the 20th Century: 1980–1989,* p. 1223.

61. Johnson, *Sleepwalking Through History,* p. 142.

Chapter Six:
Technology and Science

62. Johnson, *Sleepwalking Through History,* p. 119.

63. Quoted in Johnson, *Sleepwalking Through History,* p. 120.

64. Quoted in Johnson, *Sleepwalking Through History,* p. 121.

65. Quoted in James Wallace and Jim Erickson, *Hard Drive.* New York: John Wiley & Son, 1992, p. 230.

66. Wright, *America in the 20th Century: 1980–1989,* p. 1255.

67. Wright, *America in the 20th Century: 1980–1989,* p. 1182.

68. Quoted in David Colbert, ed., *Eyewitness to America.* New York: Pantheon Books, 1997, pp. 550–51.

Chronology

1980

Census shows 227,224,648 living in the United States.

April 24: Eight Americans die and five are injured in an attempt to rescue dozens of hostages held in the U.S. embassy in Tehran, Iran.

May 18: Mount St. Helens explodes in Washington State with a force five hundred times that of the atomic bomb dropped on Hiroshima.

November 4: Ronald Reagan becomes the fortieth president of the United States in a landslide victory over incumbent Jimmy Carter.

1981

January 20: Minutes after Ronald Reagan is sworn in, the Americans being held hostage in Iran are released.

March 30: President Reagan is shot and wounded in Washington, D.C., by John Hinckley.

April 12: The space shuttle *Columbia* lifts off on its first flight and returns safely two days later.

September 12: The nomination of Sandra Day O'Connor to become the first female U.S. Supreme Court Justice is unanimously approved by the Senate.

1982

June 12: Tens of thousands of people march in New York City against the Reagan arms buildup in the largest protest against nuclear weapons in history.

July: Proposed Equal Rights Amendment is defeated after a ten-year fight for ratification.

October 15: Ronald Reagan signs a bill deregulating the savings and loan industry.

November 5: United States records an unemployment rate of 10.4 percent—the highest since 1940.

1983

March 23: Reagan announces on national TV a new and larger defense budget and plans to build the Strategic Defense Initiative (Star Wars) weapons system.

June 18: Sally Ride becomes America's first female astronaut to travel into space when the space shuttle *Challenger* is launched.

October 23: A total of 241 U.S. Marines and sailors die in a terrorist suicide bombing in Beirut, Lebanon.

October 25: U.S. forces join Caribbean nations in invading Grenada, which was under the control of Cuban military advisers after the ouster of elected officials.

1984

March: Michael Jackson wins a record eight Grammys for the album *Thriller.*

November 6: President Ronald Reagan and Vice President George Bush are reelected in a forty-nine-state landslide victory.

1985

May: Reagan administration initiates a trade embargo against Nicaragua.

July 13: Live Aid concert, held simultaneously in London and Philadelphia, raises $70 million for starving people in Africa.

October 7: Palestinian hijackers seize the Italian cruise liner *Achille Lauro* at sea and hold four hundred hostage.

November 19–20: Reagan meets with Mikhail Gorbachev in Geneva, Switzerland, for the first superpower summit of the decade.

1986

January 20: Martin Luther King Day is first celebrated as an official national holiday.

January 28: Space shuttle *Challenger* explodes just moments after liftoff.

June 19: Len Bias, a University of Maryland basketball star, dies of a heart attack while celebrating his draft by the Boston Celtics.

October 5: A C-123 transport plane flown by Americans and carrying a cargo of jungle boots, ammunition, and rifles is shot down by the Sandinistas over Nicaragua. This event triggers the Iran-Contra investigations.

November: Public learns that the United States has sent spare parts and ammunition to Iran.

November 14: Ivan Boesky is fined $100 million and sentenced to prison for insider trading.

1987

May–August: Iran-Contra hearings are held before House and Senate committees. Reagan and Bush continue to deny knowledge, while Oliver North is assigned much of the blame for the activities in question.

October 19: "Black Monday," as the Dow Jones Industrial Average plunges 508 points after having hit a record high of 2,722 in August.

December 8: Reagan and Gorbachev agree to dismantle additional nuclear missiles.

1988

May 31: Reagan visits Moscow.

November 8: George Bush is elected the forty-first president along with running mate Dan Quayle as vice president.

1989

Census data shows 246,819,230 people living in the United States.

March 24: The *Exxon Valdez* hits a reef in Prince William Sound, Alaska, and a million gallons of crude oil is spilled over a 1,600-square-mile area, contaminating more than 800 miles of shoreline.

May 4: Oliver North is convicted of several charges related to the Iran-Contra scandal. The conviction eventually will be overturned.

June 5: In the first free Polish elections in forty years, Solidarity candidates beat Communist candidates in all districts in which they run.

August 9: Congress bails out the savings and loan industry with a bill costing $166 billion over ten years and $500 billion over thirty years.

October 17: Massive earthquake strikes San Francisco.

November 9–11: The Berlin Wall is pulled down in Germany, signaling the end of Soviet rule in Eastern Europe.

December 20: U.S. troops invade Panama and capture dictator Manuel Noriega, who surrenders on January 3, 1990. Over four thousand civilians are killed during the invasion.

For Further Reading

Bill Adler, ed., *The Uncommon Wisdom of Ronald Reagan*. Boston: Little, Brown, 1996. A book of sayings and writings by Ronald Reagan that touch on his life and presidency.

Associated Press writers, *The Reagan Era: 1981–1988;* Vol. 9 of *Twentieth Century America*, New York: Grolier Press, 1995. This series features Associated Press newspaper stories written as the news was unfolding. Good insights into the news of the Reagan era and of the Bush presidency.

————, *An Uneasy Peace: 1988– .* Vol. 10 of *Twentieth Century America*.

Ron Base and David Haslam, *The Movies of the Eighties*. London: Macdonald, 1990. This big, colorful book is an exhaustive summary of 1980s films, complete with hundreds of color pictures.

Neil Howe and Bill Strauss, *13th Gen: Abort, Retry, Ignore, Fail?* New York: Vintage Books, 1993. A revealing book of attitudes experienced and problems encountered by the so-called Generation Xers.

Haynes Johnson, *Sleepwalking Through History*. New York: Anchor Books, 1992. A fascinating roller-coaster ride through the 1980s America by a Pulitzer Prize–winning journalist.

Stuart Kallen, *Gorbachev/Yeltsin: The Fall of Communism*. Minneapolis: Abdo & Daughters, 1992. A book about the fall of the Soviet Union in the early 1990s.

————, *Retrospect of Rock*. Minneapolis: Abdo & Daughters, 1989. Details the stories of the stars behind 1980s rock and roll.

Nathan Miller, *Stealing from America*. New York: Paragon House, 1992. An exposé of government corruption from the seventeenth century to modern times.

Ronald Reagan, *An American Life*. New York: Simon & Schuster, 1990. The autobiography of the fortieth president of the United States.

Daniel A. Richman, *James E. Carter*. Ada, OK: Garrett Educational Corporation, 1989. An informative biography of America's thirty-ninth president.

David Wright, *Computers*. New York: Marshall Cavendish, 1996. A book for young adults about the history of computers and how they work. Also includes biographies of the inventors who pioneered today's computer revolution.

Works Consulted

Larry Beinhart, *American Hero*. New York: Pantheon Books, 1993. A work of fiction in which George Bush conspires with Saddam Hussein and a Hollywood film producer to make fake footage of the Persian Gulf War.

Charles S. Bullock III, James E. Anderson, and David W. Brady, *Public Policy in the Eighties*. Monterey, CA: Brooks/Cole, 1983. A scholarly work that covers the changes in social, economic, and environmental policy instituted by the Reagan administration.

Marshall B. Clinard, *Corporate Corruption*. New York: Praeger, 1990. A wide-ranging book that turns the spotlight on the unethical and illegal behavior of America's giant corporations and executives.

Leslie Cockburn, *Out of Control*. New York: Atlantic Monthly Press, 1987. The author, a producer at CBS News, traces American involvement in Nicaragua in the 1980s.

David Colbert, ed., *Eyewitness to America*. New York: Pantheon Books, 1997. A look at American history in the words of those who made it happen. The writings, gleaned from diaries, letters, memoirs, and reportage, of three hundred men and women who saw the story of America from Columbus to cyberspace.

Congressional Quarterly staff, *President Reagan*. Washington, DC: Government Printing Office, 1981. A book by the congressional editorial research and publishing service that covers the facts of Ronald Reagan's first election victory, cabinet appointments, and statements on issues, presenting biographical data as well.

Kathleen Day, *S&L Hell*. New York: W. W. Norton, 1993. A complete account of the S&L catastrophe, sparing neither the bumbling regulators nor the White House staff. Shines light on one of the biggest financial scandals in U.S. history.

Ronnie Dugger, *On Reagan*. New York: McGraw-Hill, 1983. A book about Ronald Reagan, exploring his background and presenting an analysis of his policies.

Michael Fraase, *Mac Internet Tour Guide*. Chapel Hill, NC: Ventana Press, 1993. A who, what, where, and how of the Internet that also includes the history of the Net.

William Greider, "Mandatory Minimums," *Rolling Stone,* April 16, 1998.

Roy Gutman, *Banana Diplomacy.* New York: Simon & Schuster, 1988. A behind-the-scenes look at the Reagan administration's Latin American foreign policy team, whose obsession with toppling the Sandinistas led to "freelancing" Contra aid.

Steven Levy, *Hackers: Heroes of the Computer Revolution.* Garden City, NY: Anchor Press/Doubleday, 1984. A book about the first computer hackers who emerged in the early 1970s and 1980s from university computer-science departments. They developed a technique called time sharing that provided widespread access to computers.

Janet Lowe, *The Secret Empire: How 25 Multinationals Rule the World.* Homewood, IL: Business One Irwin, 1992. A wide-ranging and compelling study of the global political-industrial-military complex that shows the impact of mega corporations on workers, consumers, and governments and how they consolidated their power in the 1980s.

Kevin Phillips, *The Politics of Rich and Poor.* New York: Random House, 1990. The author, a Republican and former Nixon staffer, uses charts, graphs, facts, and figures to show how wealthy Americans benefited during the 1980s while poor people fell further behind.

Bob Schieffer and Gary Paul Gates, *The Acting President.* New York: E. F. Dutton, 1989. An insightful book that explores the men behind Reagan and reveals how they influenced his policies. Bob Schieffer is well known as an anchor for CBS News.

Peter Schweizer, *Victory.* New York: Atlantic Monthly Press, 1994. Tells the story of a secret U.S. strategy developed by Reagan's aides that hastened the fall of the Soviet Union by undermining the Soviet economy and funneling money and weapons to its enemies. Utilizes dozens of interviews with people in the highest levels of Reagan's cabinet to show that while their policies failed to push the Soviets off the cliff, they certainly gave them a good shove.

Paul Slansky, *The Clothes Have No Emperor.* New York: Fireside Books, 1989. A humorous, no-holds-barred chronicle of the 1980s.

James B. Stewart, *Den of Thieves.* New York: Simon & Schuster, 1991. A who's who of the masterminds behind the massive wave of insider trading that was a scandal of the 1980s. Detailed backgrounds and actions of Ivan Boesky, Michael Milken, and others.

James Wallace and Jim Erickson, *Hard*

Drive. New York: John Wiley & Son, 1992. A biography of business genius Bill Gates.

Ed Ward, Geoffrey Stokes, and Ken Tucker, *Rock of Ages.* New York: Rolling Stone Press, 1986. From *Rolling Stone* magazine, a book about the history of rock and roll.

David Wright, *America in the 20th Century: 1980–1989.* New York: Marshall Cavendish, 1995. A big, easy-to-read book about all aspects of American culture during the 1980s.

Ann Wroe, *Lives, Lies, & the Iran-Contra Affair.* New York: I. B. Tauris, 1991. A look into the political scandal known as the Iran-Contra affair. Wroe is a scholar and journalist who is the American editor of the British magazine *Economist.*

Index

Picture Credits

Cover photos (from left to right): Reuters/Corbis-Bettmann, UPI/Corbis-Bettmann, UPI/Corbis-Bettmann
AP/Wide World Photos, 73 (left)
Archive Photos, 18, 24, 27, 32, 83, 89, 98
Archive Photos/Consolidated News, 31
Archive Photos/Fotos International, 81
Archive Photos/Imapress, 45
Archive Photos/Popperfoto, 108
Terry Arthur/White House Photo, 43
Ron Callaghan/Archive Photos, 69
Corbis, 15, 34
Corbis-Bettmann, 66, 68
Express Newspapers/F945/Archive Photos, 37
Bernard Gotfryd/Archive Photos, 25
Hollywood Book & Poster, 87
Jimmy Carter Library, 6
Library of Congress, 7, 59, 93
Lineworks, Inc., 30
NASA, 101, 102, 103
National Archives, 9
PhotoDisc, 48
Keith Piaseczny/Corbis-Bettmann, 64, 70
Reuters/Archive Photos, 28
Reuters/David Brauchli/Archive Photos, 35
Reuters/Corbis-Bettmann, 39 (right), 44, 55, 95 (both), 99, 105
Reuters/Nanine Hertzenbusch/Archive Photos, 107
John Springer/Corbis-Bettmann, 13
UPI/Corbis-Bettmann, 10, 21, 39 (left), 40, 47, 51, 54, 56, 57, 62, 71, 73 (right), 74, 76, 78, 80, 84, 85, 86, 91, 96, 109
Ricardo Watson/Archive Photos, 17

About the Author

Stuart A. Kallen is the author of more than 125 non-fiction books for children and young adults. He has written on topics from the 1980s ranging from Soviet history to rock and roll to the space shuttle. Mr. Kallen lives in San Diego, California.